Outcast

"The Blueprint for a Generation Seeking Purpose"

By

Prophet Keean L. Sutton

Edited By

Rebekah Elliott Mattox

Copyright 2010

OUTCAST

THE BLUEPRINT FOR A GENERATION SEEKING PURPOSE

Outcast: The Blueprint for a Generation Seeking Purpose
ISBN 978-1456391393
Printed in the United States of America

WHAT ARE PEOPLE SAYING?

"There are few books that can truly serve as a road-map in youth ministry, OUTCAST is one of them. Prophet Keean writes every word with raw passion, which leaves you wanting for more, a must read if you serve in youth ministry today." – **Joyce Kazadi**

"Outcast opened my understanding to the relevance of a shepherd and the heart of a true sheep. It's a perfect reminder of the living power of God working in us and around us even when we haven't realized it!" – **Meagan Henry**

"A must read for every leader called to bring change for this generation. This book shows God's heart and outlines His plan for this new priesthood preparing us all for the return of Christ. This book will touch the hearts of Youth Pastors and Youth Leaders across the globe, igniting revival in Youth Ministries for the 21st century." – **Adrienne Roberts**

"This book is a testament of how God changed one man's life and used him to affect the lives of many others. It is a guide for youth leaders and youth pastor's everywhere to discern the condition of this generation. If properly used, it can inspire hope and perseverance in these perilous times and for generations to come." - **Tamekia Bell**

DEDICATION

It has been a long journey for me and my family and when I thought of who to dedicate this book to I could have named several people. But there are two people God laid on my heart who have set the tone for my journey and my walk in ministry. Dalton Glenn and Patricia Pyron, you two have shown me what Christianity is all about. To Daddy Dalton, you loved me and believed in me when I did not believe in myself. You saw leadership in me when I did not see it in myself. I understand now what the legacy of a spiritual father means and the importance of a spiritual son to carry on that legacy for the great good of others. I dedicate this book to you because you have shown me that true leadership is about relationship.

To Mama Pat what can I say? You are a true woman of God who has loved not only me but everyone God has put in your path. You mean more to me then what you know, I want to say thank you from the bottom of my heart for all you have done for me, my family and my ministry. You have shown me the pathway to being a better man of God. I pray that I hold fast to the legacy in which you leave behind to us as your children. I love you with all my heart and dedicate this book to you.

To both of you, you are pillars in the ministry in which the Lord has given me and for that I will raise the banner of hope for a generation. I love you both.

TABLE OF CONTENTS

ACKNOWLEDGEMENTS

To my wife, Wynkia I want to thank you for loving me and being there for me. For allowing me to do ministry on the level that I am called to do it on, I know that my ministry does not exist without you. You are the best wife that any man can have. Thank You for all of your love and support.

To my Kids, Miracle, Josiah, and Kellan, I love you all more than you know. I pray that this book will be a map for you all when you get older and you will see what God has called you to do. With all my heart I love you.

To Adrienne, you are the reason that my ministry gets administrated and without you I could not accomplish half the work I get done on a daily basis. Thank you for helping me to push this vision to the ends of the earth. You are the best and I pray that what the Lord has laid upon me, He will also lay upon you…

To Christopher, Man what can I say about you. You have truly been a great spiritual son who has taken on the responsibility of the ministry in which the Lord has given me. Thank You for all of what you do…

To all my spiritual sons and daughters, June, Shanda, Chrystel, Marie, Damien, Yannick, Joyce, Megan, Marina, Marae, Charene, Racquel, Adrian Sims, Devon, Bria, and to all my other sons and daughters I could not name. Thank You all for believing in me and trusting the God in me to lead you to your destiny. I love you all!!!!!

To Elder Al Brown my closest friend, Thank you sir for being real, for loving God with all your heart and for pushing me to be a better leader. I thank God for you and Nena and your love for me and my family and for supporting us in our ministry journey.

To Dorothy Wilcoxson, Grandma you have always saw me as a man of God and you have believe that I would be just that. Thank You!!!!!

To Dr. Dave A. Wilcoxson (Uncle Dave) a man of true leadership, Thank you for teaching the importance of ministry, you have been a wonderful example before me.

To Bishop William Sheals (Papa), thank you for teaching me how to run God's house and how to honor it. You have always been a great example before me.

To Johnny Base, Coach Cedric, Kevin, Ms. Robin, Bobby Jackson, Keith and Muriell Davoll, Lorenzo Gonzalez, Mr. Gerald Hicks, Clayborn Knight, and Pastor White. Thank You all for being great leaders in my life. You taught me the essence of leadership and the heart of youth ministry.

To Prophet Troy Sanders, thank you for teaching me how to be a prophet, I would not be one today without your guidance and support. You have taught me the true essence of worship and that the heart of every prophet is to serve. Thank You!!!!!!

Last but not least to My Dad, Ralph Sutton, My Grandmother Betty Gray and all my siblings; Thank You all for your love. I want you all to know that I love you and that you mean the world to me. I pray that this book will serve as a legacy of our family overcoming and allowing God to use us as vessels for His generation.

FOREWORD

This foreword is for Pastor Keean's newest book, *Outcast*. Pastor Keean and I served together in American Save Our Youth program, A.S.O.Y., in conjunction with Abundant Life Christian Church of DeKalb County in Georgia. From that servitude, Pastor Keean has served as a trainer for my youth staff at Stronghold Christian Church in Lithonia Georgia when I served as the Elder over all children, youth, and young adult ministries, over the singles and all club programs including the men's' ministry for over 10 years. Pastor Keean has also served as a mediator for spiritual confrontations, and a close friend to me and my family. Our alliance and friendship spans over five years and continues to this day. His career as a man of God is impeccable, and his life as a family man is very respectable. We have walked together in each others' ministries, in retreats, in training sessions, and in matters of confidentiality. Pastor Keean is one of a couple of people outside of my Senior Pastor who are able to speak prophetically in my life.

Outcast by Pastor Keean Sutton is outstanding! There is no other way to bring to surface the unique trials that a true prophet of the God Most High has to go through. It was very enlightening to see how God develops Pastor Keean through the trials of life to become the vessel in which God uses to affect a generation. As you read this book, the weakness of Keean's life is seen as he struggles with his parents' examples, with his development from the love of baseball, to the love of a woman, and to the ultimate love of God. It was during Keean's suffering in the wilderness that he was confirmed as a prophet, which is confirmed in his marriage to Wynkia.

Outcast progresses through several dispensations to show how the enemy plans to cut off this generation's seed one by one. Keean describes our challenge in knowing the culture so we can know the God that is portrayed in this generation. With every revelation, a new demonic force has to be challenged and Keean's highlights how it affects our lives and the young people that we charged to protect. In explaining an outcast, Keean lays out their calling, purpose, vision, and mission. So many of the outcasts do not even get a chance to walk in the prophetic mantle of this generation because of the limitations put on them from their legal guardians. As Keean establishes the character of the outcasts, he vividly demonstrate the intercession, the freeing of the mind, and the setting aside that is necessary in order to fight the battles which are incorporated into this generation.

There has never been a book so candid or revealing to engross people to things going on behind the scenes in the spiritual realm. With every trial that is overcome in *Outcast*, another step to freedom for this generation is realized. As a reader, you are taken into the backyard of the spirit, shown how to anoint this generation to the kingship of the Lord, and taught how to deal with several spirits that are in operation against this generation. Pockets of resistance still persist, but Keean confers insight to how leaders are to relate to young people without entertaining them to get them to God's purpose for their lives. Once the young people realize who they are, they can begin to acquire the inactivated mantles of our spiritual forefathers for this generation. The greatest gift shown in

Outcast is the activation of mantles to get favor of God for the living army operating spiritually to bring about the Spirit of the Lord and the second coming of Jesus Christ.

Outcast is a revelatory commentary in the life of real prophet being developed by God for a generation that has lost its purpose because of untrained leaders in a generation of prophets. *Outcast* provides key insights necessary for any young adult and adult ministry to use to realize the potential in God's gifting that are already in our mist. Take an opportunity to step outside of the box and gain spiritual truth for the next generation as you read *Outcast*. The outcome will lead you to see that the outcasts are not evil, but that they are the truth means to advancing our call to prepare the way for the second coming of the Lord Jesus Christ. The end goal of this book is to help guide leaders on becoming the tools to help shape the next generation to get the full potential out of them for being activated for God. Now is the time for the true saints of God to rise up and take on the challenge of standing in the mist of adversity in order to declare the acceptable year of the Lord. There is no better way to do that besides reading your bible, studying the word of God, praying for help, and gaining knowledge from the insights and the mistakes from a man that has been proven by God—Pastor Keean and the revelations found in *Outcast*.

- Elder Alphonso Brown, Stronghold Christian Church

INTRODUCTION

The Outcast is not one who has only been rejected, but is the one chosen by God to change the world. In this time and age we need a generation to stand up and take their rightful place on the wall as watchmen. Without The Outcast understanding their position in this prophetic moment, the path of the second coming becomes held up and we become a generation lost in a time of great corruption and despair. I pray that the reader of this book will see the blue print of their life and the road map to the heart of God. In this book the outcast becomes God's end time prophet that awakens a sleeping generation from their slumber. Welcome to the "Outcast"

OUTCAST

THE BLUEPRINT FOR A GENERATION SEEKING PURPOSE

CHAPTER 1
THE OUTCAST

**"For I will restore health to you, and heal you of your wounds,"
says the Lord, "because they called you an outcast saying: this is
Zion. No one seeks her" (Jeremiah 30:17).**

It was 1994 when I moved to Atlanta from Gary, Indiana. My
purpose for moving here was to try out for the Atlanta Braves. I had
just graduated from high school, and I was confused about what I was
going to do with my life. You see, I loved baseball; it was my life, and
I could not see myself doing anything else but that. I was willing to
give up going to college *even* if that meant I would have to play *minor*
league ball! I called my father, who lived in Georgia, and I asked his
counsel about my decision. He told me I would only live once, and this
would be a great opportunity for me if I was serious about it. On
August 1, 1994, I had my bags packed and was headed towards
Atlanta, Georgia.

When I arrived in Atlanta, I looked around, and it was not like
anything I had ever seen. I grew up in the projects of Chicago, Illinois,
and both of my parents were drug addicts as well as very angry people.
When I was about thirteen years old, my dad came home for work and
caught my mom in a car with another man. My mom, knowing how
my dad was, immediately got her kids and ran in the house. She began
to put things on the door to keep him from coming in. Around
midnight, my dad came home drunk, high, and mad. My mom was

16

terrified and began to run to the back of one of the rooms. She told me, my sister, and my brother to grab the mattress and throw it out the window. As my dad broke through the window, my mom saw him and jumped from the fourth floor of our apartment. As we looked and saw our mom laying on the ground with a broken back, my dad saw her and ran. The ambulance came and picked my mom up and took her to the hospital, but my brothers, sisters, and I lay in the back of our room not knowing what would happen next. I remember lying there and praying these words, "God if you would get us out of this, I will do whatever you want me to do." The police came and gathered my siblings and me and took us next door to my Grandmother's. My dad was nowhere to be found, and we would then live with my grandmother until the courts sorted out the problems. We had not seen our dad for over six months after the incident, and I had missed him very much. My mom had gotten out of the hospital, and even though she was in pain, that did not stop her from seeking to fill her nose and veins with Crack. My dad had taken the right way out. For the six months of his absence, he had been in rehab getting himself together in order to take his kids away from a life of drugs and violence. He eventually moved us to Gary, Indiana where I would spend my high school career.

I moved to Atlanta, excited to be in a promising place, and ready to take on the passion that I so loved. My dad's friend's daughter came over to the house to meet me and some of my friends who moved here, she would bring a few of her friends as well. One of the friends to whom she introduced me would be the one who would change my life forever. As I became acquainted with her, we both could not help but to look into each other's eyes and see something special. That night, my dear readers, I fell in love. My heart was captivated by this girl. I could not get her out of my mind. Every time I would lie down, I thought about her. When I went to sleep, I thought about her. This girl had my heart, and I was crazy about her. In the mist of me falling in love with this beautiful young woman, a call came in. It was my sister from Chicago. My mom had overdosed on drugs.

My heart dropped, for the woman who gave birth to me, who loved me in her addiction, had just passed away, and I never got a chance to say goodbye. My heart was heavy and broken. My family and I flew back to Chicago to go to the funeral, but just being there made me sick. I got right back on a plane and came back to Atlanta. It was then that I knew that Atlanta would be my home. I decided at that very moment to pour my life and my heart into the girl with whom I fell in love.

She became my world, and baseball became less of my love. Soon afterwards, I walked on the baseball field to try out for the Atlanta Braves only to find myself being left on the field with broken skills. I gave up and wanted nothing else to do with baseball. I left the field in tears; my dream had left me, and a year later, the girl I fell in love with would leave me for another man. I was left alone and broken, and what I would do next, no one knew.

For six months, I chased this girl seeking the answer as to why she left me. Her reason, she said, was "church." You see, we had argued so much about my going to church that I finally ended up going. But nothing changed her mind even after I went to church; the woman I loved had left me, and my heart was full of sorrow and pain; however, something happened at church that day.

The Encounter

Church became the place where I could try and find myself and try to get her back. But God had another plan. My pain was so overwhelming that one night I drove to a church I knew about in Norcross to clear my head and heart from the pain. Upon my arrival, I saw a friend who began to minister to me about my life. Two days later, I was invited back, and it would be there that I met God; consequently, my heart was overwhelmed with great joy. I had given my heart to Jesus, and my life would never be the same.

In September of 1996, I was sitting at home wanting something to do. The night had come, and it began to rain very hard. I was intrigued by this rain because the sound of it was very different. It sounded like a voice filled with trumpets and an echo that was so angelic that it pierced my ears. The Voice came; "Keean," it said. I was very afraid of the voice and thought I was going crazy! "Keean," it said again.

**"For I will restore health to you, and heal you of your wounds,"
says the Lord, "because they called you an outcast saying: this is
Zion. No one seeks her" (Jeremiah 30:17).**

"What does that mean?" I asked. The voice came back and said these
words:

**As you come to Him, the living stone--rejected by man but chosen
by God and precious to him--you also, like living stones, are being
built into a spiritual house to be a holy priesthood, offering
spiritual sacrifices acceptable to God through Jesus Christ. For in
scripture it says: "See I lay a stone in Zion, a chosen and precious
cornerstone, and the one who trusts in Him will never be put to
shame." Now to you who believe, this stone is precious. But to
those who do not believe, the stone the builders rejected has
become the capstone and a stone that causes men to stumble and a
rock that makes them fall. They stumble because they disobey the
message which is also what they were destined for. But you are a
chosen people, a royal priesthood, a holy nation, a people
belonging to God, that you may declare the praises of Him who
called you out of darkness into his wonderful light. Once you were
not a people, but now you are the people of God. Once you had not
received mercy, but now you have received mercy" (1 Peter 2:4-
10).**

These words were very foreign to me. I did not understand what God was saying to me and why He was saying it. I did not know the voice of the Lord, but I knew it was Him talking. The voice was very piercing and so holy that I could feel God's breath all over my body. I was numb to everything that was going on around me. The Lord was talking, and I was in the mist of His Glory. I said to the Lord, "I don't understand what this means." I was instructed by Him to look up the word "outcast." Webster provided me with three different definitions:

1. A person who is stigmatized or otherwise denied the benefits of a culture, usually for being perceived as being outside the social norms of that culture.
2. A person who is rejected.
3. A person, who is unwanted, not accepted.

The Lord was very clear when He spoke to me about the word *outcast*. He said to me that this generation has been denied the benefits of the culture that He created for them and have been rejected by the church, unwanted, and not accepted in their home. "I have chosen this generation to be My Priesthood. This generation will do great things for My name's sake, and they will prepare the way for the second coming of the Lord." I was ecstatic when I learned this! The Word of the Lord had come to me, and it was very clear. The question now was, "What am I to do with this?" I never grew up in church, and I didn't know anything about ministry.

The Call of a Prophet

About a month later, after the vision of the Lord came to me, He came again and told me to leave the house in which I was living. For the next two years, I would be a homeless man. I sought shelter with a friend of mine from the church, and the Lord sent a man into my life who would help provide for me the things that I needed. Those two years were a time of teaching for me. For two years, God taught me the Word of God from Genesis to Revelation. He also made sure that I understood the identity of Holy Spirit and His purpose in the earth. He taught me the importance of prayer and said to me that I must stay in it in order to continue to grow and receive His instruction. Then He called me into the office of the Prophet. My assignment was simple; develop leaders that would have an impact on this generation. I struggled with being a prophet, especially one called to this generation. I had heard about prophets and saw what they did to people in the church. I wanted to be sincere in my heart, and genuine, when it came to the people of God especially His young people. I read 1Samuel 3:19:

"The Lord was with Samuel as he grew up, and he let none of his words fall to the ground. And all Israel from Dan to Beersheba recognized that Samuel was attested as a prophet of the Lord. The Lord continued to appear at Shiloh, and there He revealed himself to Samuel through His Word. And Samuel's word came to all Israel."

I did not want any of the words that the Lord gave me to fall to the ground. I pled with the Lord about this because it was important to my heart, and He knew it. He told me that He would honor my words and confirm them. I would now have to learn how to be a prophet.

In 1998, the Lord would send the woman of my life. She would be the one that the Lord would call to me to help me carry out the work that He put before me. My marriage was a sign that the Lord would do great things in the earth. The Lord showed himself strong at my wedding by coming down and confirming the union that He had chosen. The people became blessed by His presence, and my wife and I would begin a journey to gather the outcasts of this generation and make sure that they understood their purpose and destiny in this time.

The Sign of the Outcast

On April 20, 1999, I was in the first year of my marriage, and the unthinkable happened: One of the deadliest school shootings ever. Eric Harris and Dylan Klebold took the lives of over fifteen Columbine students in Littleton, Colorado. The nation mourned as the lives of students were lost, and tears filled the eyes of families everywhere. As the news spread, the morning newspaper read, "We did this because we were 'Outcast' in our school." My heart dropped as I read this. The Lord had confirmed His word to me, and my heart was heavy and full of pain. He spoke to my spirit and my heart: "I am preparing you to be a prophet to this generation. Go to them now. Tell them what I have called them to do." The enemy had used Eric Harris and Dylan

Klebold to destroy the hearts and lives of many young people. They had become "Outcasts" in their own schools and lives, and because of that, the young people who filled the halls of Columbine High School would become the target of the enemies plan. If you are reading this, please make note that I don't agree with what Eric Harris and Dylan Klebold did. I understand that their souls had become possessed by the mere fact that young people in social settings do not take the time to realize that the young people that they are taunting are themselves in an emotional state.

Two years after Columbine, I was sitting at home with a friend. We were watching a baseball game, and suddenly, the spirit of God took me into an open vision. In this vision, I saw the Pentagon being blown up. What actually seemed like an hour was actually only three minutes. When I came out of the vision, I told my friend what I had seen and the details of it. The date of this vision was September 10, 2001. On September 11, 2001 at 9:00a.m., I was awakened by a loud scream. It was my friend telling me to get up and turn on the TV. As I turned on the TV, I looked, and to my surprise, an airplane went into the second World Trade Center. Minutes later, breaking news came on the TV, and another airplane had crashed into the Pentagon, all in one day. In one moment, the world began to mourn the loss of hundreds of people, and many young people lost their parents. In one blow, the enemy had opened up a door that left this generation motherless and fatherless. It was with this one blow that the Lord opened up my understanding to the hand of the enemy.

CHAPTER 2

THE ANNIHILATION OF THE SEED

"Then Haman said to King Xerxes, There is a certain people dispersed and scattered among the peoples in all the provinces of your kingdom whose customs are different from those of all other people and who do not obey the king's laws; it is not in the king's best interest to tolerate them.

If it pleases the king, let a decree be issued to destroy them, and I will put ten thousand talents of silver into the royal treasury for the men who carry out this business.

So the king took his signet ring from his finger and gave to Haman son of Hammedatha, the Agagite, the enemy of the Jews." (Esther 3:8-10)

The events of September 11th were hard to swallow for a lot of people including myself. No one knew what was going on, and I was very stunned by what the Lord had shown me the day before. I needed understanding about this and why it was happening to our country and on our soil. What did this mean for us as a church, a people, and most importantly, what did this mean for our generation? As days and weeks began to come to an end, the Spirit of God spoke to me and said for me to understand the symbolism of the days and times. The Spirit told me to understand the dispensation which we are in. You may be asking yourself what the word dispensation means. Well I understand the heart and the mind of a young person, and in order for me to get you to see what God was showing me, I must define the word "dispensation."

The word "dispensation"

1. A term applying to the period of time from the coming of God's Messenger to the coming of the next Messenger.
2. A time when God gives truth to men on earth through his prophets.
3. A religious system or code of commands considered to have been divinely revealed or appointed.

The Lord wanted me to know the time of the prophetic message that he was sending out and that which He had divinely appointed. I will talk more about this in the Chapter titled "The Releasing of the Prophetic." The Lord wanted me to understand what took place on September 11, 2001. He showed me several things:

1. The month of September is the ninth month on our calendar.
2. The number nine is symbolic for birthing something out.
3. The number eleven is Symbolic for Babylon and its tower in Genesis. The number of confusion.
4. The airplane was symbolic of the demonic presence in the air.
5. And the plane hitting the Pentagon was symbolic of warfare. The Pentagon is the hub of our Military Command Center.

6. The Towers represent the towers of Babel.

7. The flames of the towers were going up on the building, and the people were jumping out of the building trying to get away from the fire by jumping right into it. This was symbolic of a people going to Hell.

On September 11, 2001, there was a birthing of a demonic influence sent here to deal with this generation. This act was more than just about America. This attack was a sign that the enemy was releasing a whole range of demonic forces in the earth to annihilate this generation. The enemy would be strategic. He would plan his attack carefully against this generation. He would take each young ones out, one by one.

A Heart to Kill

In Esther 3:8-10, you will find these words:

"Then Haman said to King Xerxes, There is a certain people dispersed and scattered among the peoples in all the provinces of your kingdom whose customs are different from those of all other people and who do not obey the king's laws; it is not in the king's best interest to tolerate them.

If it pleases the king, let a decree be issued to destroy them, and I will put ten thousand talents of silver into the royal treasury for the men who carry out this business.

So the king took his signet ring from his finger and gave to Haman son of Hammedatha, the Agagite, the enemy of the Jews."

Esther 3:8 gives us a look into the mind of a man by the name of Haman. Haman was an Agagite who wanted the seed of the Jews cut off from the face of the earth. His purpose for this goes back to King Saul, the first King of Israel. King Saul was commissioned by God to go into the Amalekites camp and kill everything that lived:

"Samuel said to Saul, I am the one the Lord sent to anoint you king over his people Israel; so listen to the message from the Lord. This what the Lord Almighty says: 'I will punish the Amalekites for what they did to Israel when they waylaid them as they came up from Egypt. Now go, attack the Amalekites and totally destroy everything that belongs to them. Do not spare them; put to death men and women, children and infants, cattle sheep, camels and donkeys." (1Samuel 15:1-3)

The Amalekites were a group of people who attacked Israel at a place called Rephidim. The purpose of this attack was to stop Israel from advancing to the Promise Land and to overtake the throne of God. God prophesied in Exodus 17:15 these words:

"For hands were lifted up to the throne of the Lord. The Lord will be at war against the Amalekites from generation to generation."

God made it a point that He would make war with the Amalekites until they were destroyed from the face of the earth. In 1Samuel 15:1-3, God sends Saul to deal with the Amalekites according to the prophetic word spoken in Exodus 17:5. When God sent Saul to deal with the Amalekites, He gave him instructions to destroy everything. God wanted nothing alive from the Amalekites because He knew that they would be trouble in the end. In 1Samuel 15:9, Saul would do the unthinkable:

"But Saul and the army spared Agag and the best of the sheep and cattle, the fat calves and lambs-everything that was good. These they were unwilling to destroy completely, but everything that was despised and weak they totally destroyed."

The mission of the generations before us was very simple; destroy all those sins and break the curse that would hinder our generation from fulfilling that in which God had appointed us to walk in. When I came into ministry, the first thing I did was read books on men and women of God in past generations who walked in the anointing of God and the things they did to keep that anointing. I wanted to know the purpose of these men and women, and what did God say to them? What did He send them to do? It was obvious that God was using them for His purpose. But what purpose was that? I became passionate about this and found myself in a world of men and women of God who had missions but no one to whom to pass it on. The generation that was at hand was caught up in sin. The world had overtaken them, and the enemy had gotten the best of them. As the forefathers told them to get rid of the sin that was before them and the sin that was in their lives, the previous generation of forefathers ignored the wisdom that was before them and continued in sin: The sexual revolution, drugs, abortion, and the list go on. Our forefathers, like Saul, did not destroy the things that God told them to destroy and left alive the bloodline that would soon give the generation to come trouble, and that's exactly what happened. In Esther 3:8-10, it reads:

"Then Haman said to King Xerxes, There is a certain people dispersed and scattered among the peoples in all the provinces of your kingdom whose customs are different from those of all other people and who do not obey the king's laws; it is not in the king's best interest to tolerate them.

If it pleases the king, let a decree be issued to destroy them, and I will put ten thousand talents of silver into the royal treasury for the men who carry out this business."

The Defilement of a Culture

Haman wanted the seed of the Jews destroyed because their culture was different from his culture and the culture of the king he served. He wanted vengeance on the seed of the Jews because of the death of his

30

great, great grandfather. Now please understand what the word "culture" means:

1. The values, traditions, norm, customs, arts, history, folklore and institutions that group a people, who are unified by race ethnicity, language, nationality or religion shared.
2. The attitudes and behaviors that is characteristic of a particular social group or organization.
3. The integration pattern of human behavior that includes thoughts, communications, actions, customs, beliefs, values and institutions of a race, ethic, religious, or social group.
4. Learned behavior of a people, which includes their belief systems and languages, their social relationships, their institutions and organizations and their institutions and organizations and their material goods, food, clothing, buildings, tools and machines.

There is a difference between the culture of this generation and the culture of the world. God created this generation in a culture of His own. This culture looks like Him, acts like Him, and smells like Him. A culture is known by the God it believes in and the values that it carries. Haman wanted the Jews killed because they did not have the belief in their God and the values of their culture. He knew that the Jews' culture would soon affect the culture that he was in. The enemy knows that this generation is here to establish a different culture than the one that has already been set before us. This culture is the culture of God. The September 11, 2001 act was all about the affecting of a culture and the killing of a seed. It was all about the shifting of the dispensation and stopping a culture from spreading to a people who need Jesus.

A Mother's Cry:

"A Canaanite woman from that vicinity came to him, crying out, Lord, Son of David, have mercy on me! My daughter is suffering terribly from demon-possession" (Matthew 15:22).

In 2000, a year before September 11, 2001, a mother walked into my job and asked my boss for me. It was strange because I had never met this woman a day in my life. I was called down to the office to meet this woman, and as I walked towards her, I could tell that she was very disturbed. I asked her what I could do for her. Her reply was, "A woman by the name of Susan Adams told me about you and your work with young people." I said, "Yes, I do work with young people."She then said to me, "My daughter is possessed by a demon." Immediately, I took a deep breath and asked the woman how she knew that her daughter was demon possessed. She looked at me and said, "While my husband and I were sleeping last night, she came into the room and tried to kill us. Her eyes were inflamed, and she did not look like our daughter." I asked the mother where her daughter was, and her mother said in the mental hospital. Anyone who has ever worked with demons before knows that when your child or anyone is possessed by a demon, you do not put them into a mental hospital, for it will only attract more demons. I told the mother to get her daughter out of there and bring her to my Friday Night Prayer Service.

An Encounter with Satan

The days passed, and the Lord had put me on a three day fast. The fast was so intense that at the end of the three days, the Lord kept me on it for four more days. Our Friday night prayer service had come, and the mother had brought her daughter. As we began to pray, the Lord had instructed me to go over to the young lady and say to the demon, "Come out!" As I shouted those words, the young lady fell to the ground, rolling on the floor. As we began to cast the demon out, one of the young ladies who was in my ministry fell to the ground. Before we knew it, we had two demons that had manifested themselves. It was crazy, and the night was just getting started. As we were dealing with the first and second demon, another demon manifested itself in a young lady. The demon threw this young lady against the wall. The demon fought as we tried to contain the young lady. Her countenance had fallen a great deal, and the demon was not just ready to let up. We had entered into warfare that was very great that day, and my body had become overwhelmed because of the fast. As we continued to deal with the demon, the third demon who had thrown the young lady against the wall, had summoned the first demon inside the mother's daughter to come to her. The young lady began to elevate off the ground. I rebuked the demon in the first young lady and put the third young lady into another room. As we wrapped up the first young lady, my mind became focused on the second young lady. We began to deal with the demons in her. The night was long, and we were nine hours into casting out these demons. The final young lady we had to deal with had come with much endurance. I was tired, and my body could not take anymore. The Lord gave me the strength to fight the battle, but these demons would not let up. We wrestled with these demons for another four hours only to leave that morning tired. The young lady would leave still having those demons inside of her. As my body began to shut down, an evil spirit came and whispered in my ear, "I am going to kill you, and there is nothing you can do about it."

The Loss of Five Sons

From that day in 1995 when I encountered the Lord, my life has been dedicated to serving Him. But nothing would be more painful than when the Lord had my wife and I walk through the loss of five sons. Our first son to be born came in 1999, a year after the Columbine shooting. We were excited, and of course, I was nervous because I had never been a father before. As we got into the first month of the pregnancy, my wife lost the baby. We were both stunned by the loss and did not understand what was going on. We asked the Lord why this had happened and the purpose of it. The Lord responded," The enemy is fighting your seed." The doctor's told us that we would not be able to have children because my wife's cervix was weak. The purpose of the cervix is to hold the baby, and the doctors were saying to me that my wife could not hold a baby. But the Lord was saying to me that the church could not hold this generation because its cervix was weak. A year passed, and my wife became pregnant again. This time, she would go six months into the pregnancy and deliver our son, Matthew, but Matthew would not make it. Matthew's name would give me insight to what the Lord was saying to me about this generation. His name means "Gift of Jehovah." God was giving this generation to the church as a gift, a gift that would change the world forever. This gift would make its mark upon the world and would be a diamond that would shine as far as Africa. My knowing all of this would not take away the pain that we were feeling. We were hurt, but our faith was alive, and it would not give in to the tactics of Satan. Two years had passed, and we lost two more babies. We began to pray and seek the face of God. I prayed to the Lord earnestly about this. And again, the Lord would be gracious to us, and she would conceive with another boy. As I began to head out to Chicago, my wife woke up about 2:00a.m. in the morning. She said to me that she was having pain. We began to pray, and in the middle of the prayer, she said she had to go to the bathroom. When she came out of the bathroom, her water broke. We rushed her to the hospital. When we got there, our son Seth had died. Tears filled my eyes, and I was overwhelmed with grief. "Why Lord?" I said. I could not take it anymore. I held my son in my hands. His eyes, his nose: he looked just like me. The spirit of God came and said, "What do you have in your hand?" I said, "My son." He said "No!" You have a dead corpse! Tell them the children have come to birth, but there is no strength to bring them forth; lift up your voice for the remnant that is left." (2Kings 19:3) I dried the tears from my eyes. I had heard from the Lord. I took this message to the church with the hope that someday we would have a child. On October 16, 2003, my wife gave birth to my beautiful daughter. We named her Miracle Elizabeth Joy Sutton. Her first name means "sign." Her middle name means "God is my oath" that is, "a worshipper of God." My daughter would be a sign that worship would become the sign of this generation. And intense worship they will walk in. How great the Lord was to us; three years later, he would give us a son. His name is Josiah Ezra Sutton. His name means "The fire of the Lord," and his middle name means "My Helper." The Lord said to me that this generation would help me carry the Fire of God to the nations. And great wonders will come through their hands. The Lord was faithful, but the hand of the enemy would be strong against this generation and would not take no for an answer.

CHAPTER 3
THE RELEASING OF THE PROPHETIC

"And it shall come to pass afterward, that I will pour out my spirit upon all flesh; and your sons and daughters shall prophesy, your old men shall dream dreams, your young men shall see visions; And also upon the servants and upon the handmaids in those days will I pour out my spirit" (Joel 2:28-29).

It was March 1998. I had been the president of my church's Youth Praise Team. It was our first anniversary, and I was very excited about it. We were having a concert to celebrate this accomplishment, and the spirit of the Lord was all over me that week. As I began to get prepared for the concert, I was taken into a vision by the spirit of the Lord. Inside the vision, I saw a great mountain. This mountain had green pastures of grass running up the side of the mountain, but the tip of the mountain was rough and filled with dirt. As I turned to the right of the mountain, I heard a noise of thundering footsteps. The footsteps were like the noise of horses running into battle. As I looked across the mountain, I saw thousands of young people coming up the mountain. These young people were clothed in all white, yet the white had dirt all over it, and some of their clothing was torn like they had been in battle. The young people in front of the line looked militant yet so holy, and I could see inside their throats the beauty of worship. They had two flags in their hands: one that said "Conquerors," and the other one that said "Jesus" written in blood. The look of these young people was not terrifying but soothing and calm. There was a presence that came from them like no other. They stood there looking over the horizon as if they had overcome, like they had been victorious in the battle that they fought. But I was left with a question: Who is this army, and why are they fighting?

The Lord's Army

"And the Lord shall utter his voice before his army; for his camp is very great; for he is strong that executeth his word." Joel 2:11

The spirit of the Lord had allowed me to see something great. I was taken into a part of the spirit to look at the generation of young people who would become the Lord's Army. It had been very clear to me over the years that this was the army I was to prepare for battle. In this preparation, the development of the army was very important. These young people could not be young people who were timid or scared to represent His name. They had to be young people like in the book of Daniel 1:3-4:

"And the King spake unto Ashpenaz the master of his eunuchs, that he should bring certain of the children of Israel and of the King's seed, and of the princes; Children in whom was no blemish, but well favoured, and skillful in all wisdom, and cunning in knowledge, and understanding science, and such as had ability in

them to stand in the king's palace, and whom they might teach the learning and the tongue of the Chaldeans."

The King wanted a group of young people who were mature enough to handle the king's business. In this maturity, the king would be able to teach them his language. This is very important because this is what the Lord wanted for His army. He wanted to be able to teach them His language. It was important that the young people who became a part of this army understood the importance of this maturity. In Joel 2:11, it says that "the Lord shall utter His voice before His army." The Lord wants His army to know two things:

1. His voice
2. The language He is speaking

The Lord's voice is what we know to be the prophetic voice of God. The word *prophetic* means the "reception and declaration of a word from the Lord." The word *reception* means the form of *receiving*, or *to receive* something, such as information, art, experience, or people. The word *declaration* means a statement that is emphatic and explicit (spoken or written). God wanted His army to receive His words and then make a statement that would be emphatic-- tending to express oneself in forceful speech or to take decisive action and explicit-fully and clearly expressed; leaving nothing implied. The Lord was very clear; the words that would be in the mouths of this army would be words of force and clearly expressed by their actions. (What they said they meant and what they did, they did with no doubt). The army that the Lord was sending was one that would execute His Word. Joel 2:11 says, " The Lord gives voice before His army, for His camp is very great; for strong is the One who executes His word." The word *execute* means to put into effect, to carry out. The army that the Lord had chosen would be the ones who:

1. Receive His Word
2. Declare His Word
3. Execute His Word

Execution is important because it tells us that this would be something that would not be easy, but it would come with a fight. The young people inside the vision had been fighting to bring forth that which God had spoken to them. The enemy had been pressing them trying to stop them from releasing the prophetic Word of God.

The Purpose for the Releasing

The greatness of the Spirit of God would be awesome, and the people who would benefit from the awesomeness of the Spirit would not be only those who would receive God's Prophetic Word but also those who would hear it. Each word of the Lord has an appointed time to be released. In this releasing, it would accomplish several things according to Hebrews 4:12

1. It would be a double edged sword.

2. It would penetrate and divide the soul from the Spirit.

3. It would judge the thoughts and attitudes of the heart.

4. It would uncover the hidden things of darkness.

The Word of the Lord would be clearly seen and heard by a generation who would open up their ears and hearts to hear and see what God was saying. The Word of the Lord was appointed for such a time as this to be released to a generation, to establish God's Kingdom, and to prepare the way for the second coming of our Lord.

As the Spirit of the Lord began to talk to me, He said that it is important for each young person to know why s/he is here--why s/he exists. In knowing this, each young person will understand the purpose of the prophetic mantle. The mantle would be one that would open up dreams and release vision for the deliverance of a people and the establishment of a kingdom here on earth. The generation in my vision understood that and was willing to die for that cause and purpose. It was here that I saw myself and thousands of other young soldiers willing to give their lives for this very cause.

The Call to Build and Tear Down
The word of the Lord came to me, saying, "Before I formed you in the womb I knew you, before you were born I set you apart; I appointed you as a prophet to the nations." "Ah, Sovereign Lord," I said, "I do not know how to speak; I am only a child."

But the Lord said to me, "Do not say, 'I am only a child.' You must go to everyone I send you to and say whatever I command you. Do not be afraid of them, for I am with you and will rescue you," declares the Lord. Then the Lord reached out his hand and touched my mouth and said to me, "Now, I have put my words in your mouth. See, today I appoint you over nations and kingdoms to uproot and tear down, to destroy and overthrow, to build and to plant" (Jeremiah 1:4-10).

We see three things in these verses of Jeremiah:

1. Before Jeremiah was formed in his mother's womb, God knew him.
2. Before Jeremiah was born, God set him apart.
3. God appointed him to be a prophet to the nations.

Before Jeremiah was formed, God knew him. God's thoughts of Jeremiah were for a specific plan, purpose, and destiny. God wanted a young man who would shape and carry His word to the nations. He wanted this person to exalt His name, His Kingdom, and His purpose. So God named the young man Jeremiah which means "Jehovah high and exalted of God." Before Jeremiah would come out of his mother's womb, God would set Jeremiah apart for this task. The only thing is Jeremiah would not know of this call until the right time and moment. His appointment would be to the office of the prophet. He would be God's mouthpiece; he would be God's seer. His mission included six assignments:

1. To uproot kingdoms
2. To tear down kingdoms
3. To destroy kingdoms
4. To overthrow kingdoms
5. To build a kingdom
6. To plant a kingdom

The mission of Jeremiah was very important because, as you can see, he would deal with three things:

1. The heart of man
2. The nations
3. The kingdoms of those nations

God wanted a young person who could uproot, tear down, destroy and overthrow kingdoms. He wanted a generation that could go in and build and plant His Kingdom. This generation had to be kingdom-minded. But in order for them to be kingdom minded, they had to know the mind of the King. The generation that I saw in the vision sat with God for years before their time of release, learning from God His mind and heart. Like the disciple in Luke 24:44-45, Jesus said these words to them:

"He said to them, 'This is what I told you while I was still with you: Everything must be fulfilled that is written about me in the Law of Moses, the Prophets and the Psalms.' Then He opened their minds so they could understand the Scriptures."

As this generation sat with God in this vision, God began to open their minds to the scriptures and give them great understanding of the times to be fulfilled. In Luke 24:32, the disciples said these words about the opening of their understanding:

"They asked each other, "Were not our hearts burning within us while he talked with us on the road and opened the Scriptures to us?""

Like a flame in the hearts of the disciples, so the hearts of this generation would be as God would open up their understanding to the scriptures. They would become like Jeremiah in Jeremiah 20:7-9:

"O Lord, you deceived me, and I was deceived; you overpowered me and prevailed. I am ridiculed all day long; everyone mocks me.

Whenever I speak, I cry out proclaiming violence and destruction. So the word of the Lord has brought me insult and reproach all day long.

But if I say, 'I will not mention him or speak any more in his name,' his word is in my heart like a fire, a fire shut up in my bones. I am weary of holding it in; indeed, I cannot."

The Mysteries of God:

"He answered and said to them, 'Because it has been given to you to know the mysteries of the kingdom of heaven, but to them it has not been given. For whoever has, to him more will be given, and he will have abundance; but whoever does not have, even what he has will be taken away from him. Therefore I speak to them in parables, because seeing they do not see, and hearing they do not hear, nor do they understand. And in them the prophecy of Isaiah is fulfilled, which says: 'Hearing you will hear and shall not understand, And seeing you will see and not perceive; For the hearts of this people have grown dull. Their ears are hard of hearing, And their eyes they have closed, Lest they should see with their eyes and hear with their ears, Lest they should understand with their hearts and turn, So that I should heal them.' "But blessed are your eyes for they see, and your ears for they hear; for assuredly, I say to you that many prophets and righteous men desired to see what you see, and did not see it, and to hear what you hear, and did not hear'" (Matthew 13:11-17).

The Spirit of the Lord spoke to me in 2006 and said to me, "It has been given to you to know the mysteries of the Kingdom of Heaven..." "What does this mean?" I asked the Lord? I learned that the word *mystery* in Greek is "muo" which means "secrets." Psalm 24:14 says, "The secret of the Lord is with them that fear him; and he will shew them his covenant." The Lord said to my heart, "I am bringing a generation into a realm of the spirit where I will begin to unlock the secrets which I have had stored up since the beginning. There is a time for these secrets to be released, and it will only be released to the generation that has been ordained to unlock those mysteries in the time which I have ordained for them to be released."

Remember in Chapter 2, "The Annihilation of the Seed," I talked about the word "dispensation." Now let me give you the meaning of the word "dispensation." The word "dispensation" is a term referring to the period of time from the coming of God's Messenger to the coming of the next Messenger. It is a time when God gives Truth to men on earth through His prophets; it further means a religious system or code of commands considered to have been divinely revealed or appointed.

Amos 3:7 says, "Surely the Lord God does nothing, unless He reveals His secret to His servants the prophets." One thing the Lord wanted me to understand was that He would do nothing in the earth until those that He prophetically called would come forth. Ephesians 1:3-10:

"Blessed be the God and Father of our Lord Jesus Christ, who has blessed us with every spiritual blessing in the heavenly places in Christ, just as He chose us in Him before the foundation of the world, that we should be holy and without blame before Him in love, having predestined us to adoption as sons by Jesus Christ to Himself, according to the good pleasure of His will, to the praise of the glory of His grace, by which He has made us accepted in the Beloved. In Him we have redemption through His blood, the forgiveness of sins, according to the riches of His grace which He made to abound toward us in all wisdom and prudence, having made known to us the mystery of His will, according to His good pleasure which He purposed in Himself, that in the dispensation of the fullness of the times He might gather together in one all things in Christ, both which are in heaven and which are on earth--in Him."

The young people in this dispensation have been predestined to unlock the mysteries of the will of God. The purpose of our unlocking these secrets is to bring together all things in Christ. What do I mean by *all things*? In Romans 8:19, it says:

"The creation waits in eager expectation for the sons of God to be revealed. For the creation was subjected to frustration, not by its own choice, but by the will of the one subjected it, in hope that the creation itself will be liberated from its bondage to decay and

brought into the glorious freedom of the children of God. We know that the whole creation has been groaning as in the pains of child birth right up to the present time."...

All of God's creation has been taken captive by the bondage of this world. There are families, lands, nations, people, and kingdoms that have been taken captive by the bondage of the enemy. Each generation has been called to set at liberty those things that have been taken into bondage by the hand of the enemy through the prophetic voice of that generation. Creation waits for those sons and daughters to be born and then to speak. Creation cannot be set free until those sons and daughters who have been born in that generation are revealed. Until those sons and daughters come forth, creation will sit in frustration causing all creation to go haywire. When Jesus came on the scene, He said these words:

"The Spirit of the Lord is upon Me, Because He has anointed me to preach the gospel to the poor; He has sent Me to heal the brokenhearted to proclaim liberty to the captives and recovery of sight to the blind, to set at liberty those who are oppressed; To proclaim the acceptable year of the Lord"
(Luke 4:18-19).

Creation waits for us to come forth because the Lord has need of that which He has created to be used for His glory. I understand this more and more as I continue on my journey in life. I have been appointed to speak in this hour; you have been appointed to speak in this hour. The mysteries of God are vital to the releasing of this generation and setting the tone for the second coming of our Lord and Savior Jesus Christ. If this generation does not speak, it holds back our Lord from returning.

The Mysteries Finished

"I saw still another mighty angel coming down from heaven, clothed with a cloud. And a rainbow was on his head; his face was like the sun, and his feet like pillars of fire. He had a little book open in his hand. And he set his right foot on the sea and his left foot on the land, and cried with a loud voice, as when a lion roars. When he cried out, seven thunders uttered their voices. Now when the seven thunders uttered their voices, I was about to write; but I heard a voice from heaven saying to me, "Seal up the things which the seven thunders uttered, and do not write them." The angel whom I saw standing on the sea and on the land raised up his hand to heaven and swore by Him who lives forever and ever, who created heaven and the things that are in it, the earth and the things that are in it, and the sea and the things that are in it, that there should be delay no longer, but in the days of the sounding of the seventh angel, when he is about to sound, the mystery of God would be finished, as He declared to His servants the prophets.

Then the voice which I heard from heaven spoke to me again and said, "Go, take the little book which is open in the hand of the angel who stands on the sea and on the earth." So I went to the angel and said to him, "Give me the little book." And he said to me, "Take and eat it; and it will make your stomach bitter, but it will be as sweet as honey in your mouth." Then I took the little book out of the angel's hand and ate it, and it was as sweet as honey in my mouth. But when I had eaten it, my stomach became bitter. And he said to me, "You must prophesy again about many peoples, nations, tongues, and kings" (Revelation 10).

Now I know that you may be saying that this is a long scripture, but the scripture is there for a purpose, and I want you to understand what the Lord has been saying. In the year that the Lord spoke to me about the mysteries of God, He said to me that the Lord Jesus would not come back until the prophets of the dispensation finished speaking that which is locked up in the Spirit. The Angel in Revelation 10 stands between the sea and land and intercedes on behalf of the earth. When this happens, seven thunders utter their voices. Whenever you see "thunders" like this in scripture, it means that God is getting ready to speak, and that is just what He does in this scripture. God begins to speak from the depth of the angel's intercession.

When John heard this, God told him to seal up what he had heard. This is symbolic of the locking up of the mysteries that the Lord has stored up. God tells him that the time will come when that which He has revealed will come to an end, but there must be a servant who will speak those mysteries. That's what the Lord is saying to us: the mysteries of God must come to an end. We as a generation must prophesy that which has been locked up. Nothing will come to an end until that which is locked up has been spoken and manifested. Only then will God come back for His people.

The Valley

"So I prophesied as he commanded me, and breath entered them; they came to life and stood up on their feet--a vast army" (Ezekiel 37:10).

The Spirit of the Lord took Ezekiel into a valley. Inside this valley were bones laying everywhere. The problem with this valley is that it was full of soldiers who fought a battle but lost it because of their spiritual condition. This is the same valley that the Lord has allowed me to see concerning this generation and those to come.

The Lord asked Ezekiel, "Can these bones which are dead, can they live again?" Ezekiel's response was, "Lord, only you know." My heart has been beating deeply with this response as the Lord pushes us closer to this generation. My ear has become sensitive to the fact that we have come to a generation whose eyes are fixed on that which is material and not that which is of the Spirit. The eyes of our generation are fixed on the fabulous life of the rich and famous and the pursuit of how "I can be down." Hip Hop has taken this generation to a whole other level cashing in on the pain and arrogance of a generation who says it knows God, but it does not know His ways.

At this very moment, a four year girl is learning how to be the next big thing in the hip hop industry by emulating the top music videos. This generation in number is more than any other generation on earth, and the valley where they live has become the place of their graves. We can't make a young person understand the dispensation in which s/he lives, nor can we question the value system of which s/he believes because we can't be heard through deceived ears in bondage.

I was invited to speak at a Watch Night Service in December 2005. As I began to consecrate myself that week, the Holy Spirit came to me and said, "Something greater than Hip Hop is coming." The minute I said this, young people in the crowd began to boo and hiss me! The whole place erupted, and I was left there with a bunch of young people who were captive to that which they had been listening. Their hearts and minds had been taken over by a culture that promoted rebellion, and they were in awe to know that they were going to lose that. My heart was broken and disturbed at this point. I asked, "What is this Lord?" God replied, "You are looking at the army that I have chosen to be ambassadors for My Kingdom."

Like Ezekiel, I was brought to a valley to see a culture, a people, an army that lay there dead. This army could not move; it had not yet been put together. This army could not speak; it had no life. This army could not move because it had not been called forth and commissioned to move. Like Ezekiel, I was commanded by God to prophesy to a generation. I was commanded to look and to see a generation come forth. I was commanded to see the Lord's Army. I was questioning, "If this is your Army, Lord, who will believe it?" This generation has proven that it is not ready to handle the anointing that the Lord has been ready to put on their individual lives. But through all of what I saw, and no matter what anyone thinks, the Lord is ready to prepare His Army for battle. He is ready to bring forth the Army. When will the Army become ready?

CHAPTER 4
THE LOST PROPHETS

"I brought you up out of Egypt, and I led you forty years in the desert to give you the land of the Amorites. I also raised up prophets from among your sons and Nazirites from among your young men. Is this not true, people of Israel?" declares the Lord."But you made the Nazirites drink wine and commanded the prophets not to prophesy"(Amos 2:10-12).

I now understand more about the Lord's will than I ever have before on my journey with Him. But I must tell you the truth: this section of this book shakes me up very badly! The Lord's desire to see a generation raised up for the glory of the Kingdom has possessed my heart and rendered it to the purpose of the Kingdom. However, many don't understand the significance of a generation being raised up to unlock the mysteries of the Kingdom of God. My journey to bring forth a message to a generation has caused me great persecution and dirt thrown in my face. The Lord was clear to me that I was to train and to equip His generation for the work of the ministry and to bring them to a place where they understood The Prophetic Call. This meant developing an atmosphere where I could do this and not be ashamed of the training. Consequently, in the year 2000, I started to allow young people to stay with me in my home as they graduated from high school. It would be here that I would be able to pour into them everything I knew about the vision and mission of the generation and begin to biblically prepare them for the hand of the enemy. I was excited about the opportunity that was given to me but a lot of parents were not! I began to receive messages that I was stealing the kids away from their parents, and that I had too much influence over them. This message put a dagger in my heart, for it was never my intention to neither steal nor lead a young adult down the wrong path. My assignment was simple: raise up a generation of young people for God's glory.

The influence I had came not on my own accord, but was the influence of the Holy Spirit. He told me to just speak, and He would do the rest. I had been labeled by a few parents, yet there were many who understood my purpose in their children's lives. For some, I was a blessing; to others, I was a curse. The parents who considered me to be a curse wanted their children to have a life of wealth--to be what they wanted them to be and not who God had created them to be. To my opposition, for a young person to be so deeply involved in church was absurd and just too much; it was inconceivable: no young person could ever be out until two o'clock in the morning in a prayer meeting or out of town helping reach lost souls for the Kingdom! Many parents did not want their children involved in church that much. They just wanted them to be there on Sunday's and to pursue the American Dream. The Lord was not OK with this, and He wanted more from this generation. He wanted more from His young people than just to be mediocre and to do what everyone else was doing. He had created them for something great. If they were to get caught up into thinking that having material things, riches, and the American dream was the way, then they would have missed the purpose for their lives. It is the responsibility of every parent to realize what the Lord has called their children to do on the earth. Like Hannah in 1 Samuel 1:26-28,

"And she said to him, "As surely as you live, my lord, I am the woman who stood here beside you praying to the LORD. I prayed for this child, and the LORD has granted me what I asked of him. So now I give him to the LORD. For his whole life he will be given over to the LORD." And he worshiped the LORD there".

Hannah understood that her child had been given to her for purpose and it was her job to prepare him for it. Hannah had begun to wean young Samuel. The word "wean" according to Webster means to accustom an infant or small child to food other than a mother's milk or bottle. In this one definition we find the drive of Hannah's heart. She had to prepare her son to live without her; she had to prepare him to walk before the Lord. She had to prepare him to understand that he was no ordinary child. He had Destiny! We as parents have to prepare our children to do what the Lord has called them to do; to prepare them to stand before the Lord and take upon His assignment. Only then will our children live out greatness.

Mary the Carrier of Purpose

In the sixth month, God sent the angel Gabriel to Nazareth, a town in Galilee, to a virgin pledged to be married to a man named Joseph, a descendant of David. The virgin's name was Mary. The angel went to her and said, "Greetings, you who are highly favored! The Lord is with you." Mary was greatly troubled at his words and wondered what kind of greeting this might be. But the angel said to her, "Do not be afraid, Mary, you have found favor with God. You will be with child and give birth to a son, and you are to give him the name Jesus. He will be great and will be called the Son of the Most High. The Lord God will give him the throne of his father David, and he will reign over the house of Jacob forever; his kingdom will never end." "How will this be," Mary asked the angel, "since I am a virgin?" The angel answered, "The Holy Spirit will come upon you, and the power of the Most High will overshadow you. So the holy one to be born will be called the Son of God." Luke 1:26-35

It had been very evident to me that the Lord was calling this generation to do something greater than their parents could even imagine. This would be most evident in one parent who understood that her son had been called for a deeper purpose even if she did not understand it all.

Sonya Chapman, a woman of great faith, and a deep passion for worship, had birthed one of the greatest leaders, I believe of this generation. Like any mother, Sonya's son, Christopher Williams, was the beat of her heart. He was her first born and she knew the Lord had His hand upon him. Christopher was a gifted athlete and an excellent student but Mrs. Chapman was adamant about understanding the Lord's call on her son's life even if she did not fully understand the process. Christopher Williams would become the Assistant Pastor of Vigor Youth Ministries and become one of my frontline leaders. Like many mothers before her, Mrs. Chapman had become the carrier of purpose and it was her job to say "be it unto me Lord according to your word" even if she did not understand it all.

Every parent must know that they won't understand the process that their children must go through to fulfill their call. They must expect that there is a process, but more importantly there is purpose. It is the parent's job to make sure that the child understands that they have been consecrated unto the Lord and birthed for His purpose. We must be careful on what we allow them to engage in. Their choices may be detrimental to their call and their purpose.

No one understood this more than Mary as she had to prepare her Son to carry all humanity on His shoulders. She had to watch her Son be beaten and then nailed to a wooden cross. She was in agony yet she understood that He had to go through this. It was His destiny.

Like the children of Israel in Amos chapter 2, many parents have held their children back from becoming who God intended for them to be. I do not say this to bash the parent, for I know that all parents love their children with all their hearts, but every parent must see their children for who they were created to be. We must understand that the plan of the Lord is the plan that will sustain our children's lives and not our own plan. The children of Israel caused their children, who were called to be Prophets and Nazarites, to be silent in a time when God was speaking. They caused their children who were called to be Nazarites, to drink the wine of defiled cultures. These incidents caused many people in Israel to fall and to go astray, and the Lord was not pleased with it. His judgment was coming upon Israel, and He would not stop until He got justice for His Prophets and the Nazarites. The Lord was speaking very clearly to me. He would judge those who did not release His young prophets, and He would deal with those who have led those young people, who have been called to a life of consecration and prayer, away from what they were called to do. For the Lord would not allow another Prophet to be lost or another Nazarite to be defiled.

CHAPTER 5

THE RISE OF CHRIST'S PRIESTHOOD

"Then Moses went up to God, and the Lord called to him from the mountain and said, This is what you are to say to the house of Jacob and what you are to tell the people of Israel: 'You yourselves have seen what I did to Egypt, and how I carried you on eagles' wings and brought you to myself. Now if you obey me fully and keep my Covenant, then out of all nations you will be my treasured possession. Although the whole earth I mine. You will be for me a kingdom of priests and a holy nation. These are the words you are to speak to the Israelites" (Exodus 19:1-6).

In 2005, I had been in my prayer chambers praying and studying my Bible. I came across these words in the book of Exodus, "You will be for me a kingdom of Priests and a holy nation. These are the words you are to speak to the Israelites." When I read these words, the Lord said to me, "Tell them that they are going to be for Me a Kingdom of Priests." Now these words meant a lot to My Lord, and yes, they became the drive of my heart. I was to tell a generation that God was calling them into priesthood--not just any old Priesthood, but the Priesthood of Christ. This meant that a generation had to get prepared to take on the mission and the assignment of Christ, and they could not be held up by the affairs of this world. This could not be just any priesthood; this had to be a priesthood that was willing to take on the challenge of fulfilling what the Lord had laid out for them and they had to be willing to lay down their lives for a cause greater than themselves. They had to give up their lives for their generation. Now there are some things that I need to explain to you in order for you to understand what the Lord wanted from his Priests. The first thing you need to know is what a priest is. A priest is one who engages in holy matters. The Hebrew word means "Bridge-Builder." The priests were to be mediators between God and man. According to *Tyndale Bible Dictionary,* priests were servants of God in the Old Testament. This was not an occupation considered of professional living, but rather a response to a specific call of God.

What is the Purpose of the Priest?

The Priests were responsible for declaring God's will to the people, teaching God's ordinances and laws, and they served in the tabernacle by offering sacrifices and intercession for the Children of Israel. They were called to live a consecrated life set apart from others so God might use them to restore proper worship and relationship with Him. Priests were responsible for bearing the sins of the people and making intercession on their behalf to God.

What is the Character of the Priest?

Before we can understand the character of a priest, we must first understand what character is. Character can be defined as beyond usual; completeness of whom one was, is, and will be. Thomas McCauley says that "Character is what a man would do if he would not be found out." For us, Character is a quality or trait that distinguishes an individual or group. Herbert Spencer says: "Character is the inherent complex of attributes that determine a person's moral and ethical actions and reactions."

So if we could break this down in the context of a priest, we would say that a priest is one who engages in holy matters; with qualities and requirements that are beyond the usual. They are not like the general population. Their character determines how people think, behave, and govern themselves. It is the completeness of attributes that dictate their beliefs, which influences their actions and reactions to the outside world.

When God called the Children of Israel to the Mountain, He was calling them to prepare them for one of the greatest works ever. The first thing they had to know was who they were. They were called to be priests, and in that, God had to prepare them. They did not have the character to carry the assignment of a priest because they had lived in Egypt for four hundred years. So when God called them to the mountain, He had to break a slave mindset and get the people to understand who they were. This is the challenge that we have as youth pastors as we launch out to free a generation from the mindset of being slaves to sin. God has called this Generation to be His priests and to engage in a holy cause that will prepare the way of the second coming of the Lord. This generation will be responsible for:

1. Re-establishing prayer in the earth
2. Re-establishing God's Word and teaching it to every nation
3. Lead the nations of this world back to proper worship
4. Reconcile a generation to God, its Father, by proclaiming Jesus and ministering in the power of the Holy Spirit.

Israel could not do this if they did not go through the necessary process of having their hearts purged and their minds renewed. For four hundred years, the children of Israel had been in bondage to Egypt. Now, I want you to understand the prophetic symbolisms of Egypt and to this generation. Egypt is known for its great wealth and prestige. It was known for its ability to provide the nations around it with substance and resources. Here, Egypt is a shadow type of the World System. Pharaoh, Egypt's king, is known for being the god of Egypt. He was the life of Egypt, the breath of Egypt's being, and he personified the gods of Egypt. A picture of Pharaoh's crown is a golden crown with a serpent placed in the middle of it. This is a shadow type of Satan ruling the world. Our generation has been in bondage to the world system for years, and God has come to set them free in order to prepare them for his mandate and mission. When God called Israel to the mountain, He called them there to reveal to them who they were going to be and the mandate and mission upon which they had to embark. But before God could do any of that, He had to strip their hearts and minds from four hundred years of strong, intense bondage. The Lord said to me that "the generation that is in your eyesight must go through the process of being purged from the heart and mindset of the world in order to carry the mantle of the priest." He told Moses, "Go to the people and consecrate them today and tomorrow. Have them wash their clothes and be ready by the third day because on that day, the Lord will come down on Mount Sinai in the sight of all the people" (Exodus 19: 10-11).

The Lord today has sent instructions to the Youth Pastors and Youth Leaders who have been called to be today's Moses. He says to you, "Consecrate the generation and get them prepared for today and tomorrow." The washing of their clothes signifies the changing of their garments. That which is of the old will be washed and prepared for that which will be new. The Lord has said to us that the preparation of this generation is so important. The church has lost sight of this. Our preparation has been giving this generation entertainment and filling them up with every kind of desire that will draw them to attend our youth groups or youth ministry. This has taken away from a generation being washed for the preparation to meet the Lord and has left a generation with an imitation of the presence of God. With this being said, it is important that we get an understanding of what the Lord is saying concerning this generation and to what He is calling them. Israel's call to the mountain was a call of urgency, and God wanted to make sure that they understood that urgency. He was calling them to the mountain to push them and to prepare them to handle one of the greatest worship experiences ever. They would have the privilege of learning how to come before God and how to teach those around them to do the same, but this was just part of the preparation. They were called to the mountain to get prepared to carry out the vision that God revealed to their forefathers. In Genesis 15:12-16, you will read:

"As the sun was setting, Abram fell into a deep sleep, and a thick and dreadful darkness came over him.
Then the Lord said to him, "Know for certain that your descendants will be strangers in a country not their own, and they will be enslaved and mistreated four hundred years.
But I will punish the nation they serve as slaves, and afterward they will come out with great possessions.
You, however, will go to your fathers in peace and be buried at a good old age.
In the fourth generation your descendants will come back here, for the sin of the Amorites has not yet reached its full measure."

The part of this section that I want you to focus on is the last verse. In Genesis 15:16, it says that "In the fourth generation your descendants will come back here, for the sin of the Amorites has not yet reached its full measure." That year, the Lord spoke to me and said that He was ready to bring forth a priesthood that would deal with the sins of the enemy. God was pulling a generation from bondage to deal with the enemy. This is why we as youth pastors and leaders are to prepare a generation to meet the Lord: to bring them to the mountain by the Lord's command and to prepare them to understand the assignment on which they must embark. When this happens, a generation will be prepared, and Priesthood will arise.

CHAPTER 6

THE ANOINTING OF A KING

"So he sent and had him brought in. He was ruddy, with a fine appearance and handsome features. Then the Lord said, "Rise and anoint him; he is the one. So Samuel took the horn of oil and anointed him in the presence of his brothers, and from that day on the Spirit of the Lord came upon David in power. Samuel then went to Ramah" (1 Samuel 16:12-13).

The year 2007 came, and as I was sitting in my chambers, the word of the Lord came to me and said, "Arise and anoint Me a King." In 2006, my ministry had implemented a two year program for youth ministries in the state of Georgia. It was in this two year program that the Lord would look for those He was calling to be a part of what we know to be Joel's Army. This would prove to be hard for me as a prophet to this generation. Five churches became a part of this two year training, and once we got started, two of them dropped out. We began with a hundred young people, and by the end of the two years, we were down to thirty. In October of 2007 as I sat in my chambers, the Lord said to me," Arise and anoint me a King." He said to me, "These few who stand here are the beginning of Joel's Army. They will be the priests I use to bring back proper worship and the bridge-builders between the forefathers and their generation, but they will also be anointed as My Kings in the earth bringing forth My Kingdom and establishing it here on the earth." The problem was could these young people be the kings for whom the Lord was looking? I had been hard on these young people for two years, and I had become frustrated that they would not live up to what the Lord was calling them to do and to be. In my mind, I thought, "Do they understand the depth of that which the Lord is calling them to? Do they understand the importance of reaching a generation of young people and establishing the Kingdom of God here on Earth? I was stuck.

That October, we were holding our Intense Worship Service, and I knew what the Lord had said to me, but who would really be the ones that would carry the Kingship? I stepped to the podium, and my assignment that day was not to anoint them but to prepare them for the anointing. Like Samuel, I had become shaky about who would be the ones. When Samuel approached Jesse's house, seven of Jesse's sons had been there, and they all looked good. The problem with Samuel was that as he went to the house, he got caught up in the way they looked. This is the problem with eighty per cent of the youth pastors in this generation. They are caught up in the way the young people look and the way their youth ministries should be. The Lord was not concerned about that. His statement to Samuel was this: "But the Lord said to Samuel, 'Do not consider his appearance or his height, for I have rejected him. The Lord does not look at the things man looks at. Man looks at the outward appearance, but the Lord looks at the heart.'" The outward appearances of our young people and our youth ministries are not important to the Lord right now. The first thing the Lord was looking for in His King was the passion and the obedience of his heart. I had to look for this inside the young people to whom the Lord was calling me. Did they have the passion, and did they have the ability to be obedient? Samuel had to go back to the drawing board, and if I was not careful in my search, I would be right there with Samuel. He was confused: "Lord did you send me here just to find no king?" So it was for me. As a prophet, I stood before those young people not knowing whether or not they would be the ones to survive the cut. But Samuel said to Jesse, "Are these all the sons you have?" (1 Samuel 16:11). "There are more sons and daughters out there," the Lord was saying to me. You must be able to pick that up in the spirit realm and youth pastors and youth leaders must be able to pick this up, to discern this, in the spirit realm. These young people are not in the house of carnality but in the backyard of the spirit. Jesse said to Samuel, "There is still the youngest," Jesse answered, "but he is tending the sheep" (1 Samuel 16:11). The question the Lord had for me was, "Can the young people I choose tend sheep?" The sheep were important to the Lord because His King had to be sensitive to the sheep and know how to take care of them. These young people will catch the Lord's heart. Samuel said to Jesse, "Send for him; we will not sit down until he arrives"(1Samuel 16:11). The Lord said to me, "They have sat down before the generation that I have chosen and have come in to be confirmed by the Prophet." Youth pastors, youth leaders, senior pastors, and governments have missed a generation of young people because they have sat down only to show dishonor to that generation.

As I write this chapter, even I, like David, have struggled with this simple desire. What does it take to be a son? David's job was the lowest of them all: he was a shepherd. While his brothers enjoyed the good life and the favor of their father, David was put out of the house to tend his father's sheep. In the eyes of his father and brothers, this was a job for the rejected, the stupid, and the wasted, but in God's eyes, it was the highest position in the Kingdom. Right now, there is a young person who has been faithful over that which God has given him/her. S/he has stayed away from trying to be like everyone else accepting the fact of being different from everyone in the house, and even though s/he has been put out of the house to tend the sheep, his/her heart is full of joy because of knowing of the soon-to-come anointing as God's King or Queen. David walked through the door of the house with everyone's eyes fixed on him. The prophet Samuel, with his horn full of oil, looked upon a young man who smelled like sheep, and who looked like he had been wrestling to keep the flock alive. To the young people who have been fighting to keep their youth ministries alive, to the young people who have been on their knees crying out for their generation and praying for revival to come to their cities or to their schools and to their homes, this is what the Lord has decreed. To the Youth Pastors, Youth Leaders, and prophets all around this world, "Rise and anoint him; he is the one." This generation has been chosen by the Lord to carry His people to place where He has ordained for them to go. It is with this prophetic word in my belly and in my hearing that I search out a generation of young people who have been passionately in pursuit of His Name, to help establish His Kingdom; for you, the Lord is getting ready to anoint in the presence of your brethren, those who passed by the prophet but did not have the heart of the Lord. For this reason, the Lord has raised me and other soldiers to come with our horns full of oil to anoint a generation for Kingship!

CHAPTER 7
THE SPIRIT OF JUDAS

"When Jesus had said these things, He was trouble in spirit, and testified and said, "Most assuredly I say to you, one of you will betray Me." Then the disciple looked at one another, perplexed about whom He spoke.

Now there was leaning on Jesus' bosom one of His disciples, whom Jesus loved. Simon Peter therefore motioned to him to ask who it was of whom He spoke. Then, leaning back on Jesus' breast, he said to Him, "Lord, who is it?" Jesus answered, "It is he to whom I shall give a piece of bread when I have dipped it." And having dipped the bread, He gave it to Judas Iscariot, the son of Simon. Now after the piece of bread, Satan entered him. Then Jesus said to him, "What you do quickly"(John 13:21-27).

In 1995, when the Lord called me, I was very excited. Although I did not understand everything, I knew that the Lord chose me to bring revival to a generation. I knew that I had to prepare myself as well as prepare them to hold the revival that God was calling me to spread. I will talk more about this in the Chapter "Revival Fire." The Lord knew that I had to bring this about, but the pain that He would allow me to go through would be great. As I was coming up through the development of my ministry, I found myself being hurt by those inside of the ministry that God had called me to. People were telling me to put youth ministry down, and I was being "lied on" by those inside the circle of leadership. I could not trust anyone, and everyone whom I could not trust found themselves fighting with each other. I was in a ministry where gossip and backbiting became the pillar, and the young people around us had felt the effects of it all. I had set up a meeting with my Senior Pastor not to complain about what was going on in the youth ministry but to let him know that I had received a call from God and was ready to take the next step into that ministry. My Senior Pastor confirmed my ministry and put me into what he called "the wilderness." I love this because it is here that one finds out if s/he is really called to ministry. For two years, I sat in the wilderness, and the enemy was coming at me hard! The youth ministry at the church that I was a part of birthed more wickedness, and the spiritual condition of the young people was getting worse. I had become irritated and was frustrated about what was going on. A staff meeting was called for the youth leadership staff, and I was going to voice my concerns for the youth. As the meeting began, we started to discuss the problems. The Youth Pastor walked in the meeting, and he was very angry. He began to rebuke us, but all his attention was mainly coming at me. I was labeled a "rebel" and an "outcast" and was told that I would not be licensed. I began to lash out at him calling his character on the carpet. Leaders from both ends of the table grabbed us as we were almost at each other's necks. I was put out of the meeting and went to my car crying. I was upset, and those around me had been talking about kicking me out of the youth ministry because of a lie. I knew that this was wicked and wrong. All I cared about was serving the young people, and now, the leadership had labeled me a trouble maker. I was suspended from the youth ministry for two weeks for "going off on" the youth pastor. I could not bear to see myself back at the church among the young people. I stayed at home for three months praying and asking God, "Why did this happen?" I was ready to leave the church and go back to the world. During a night in the third month of my refuge, the Lord came to me and began to talk to me. Like Elijah, He asked me, "Why are you here?" I said, "The Youth Pastor and leaders have conjured up a lie against me and I cannot face the young people any longer." The Lord, at that point, began to rebuke me about the anointing on the Youth Pastor's life and how I was to value that anointing no matter what the Youth Pastor had done. He said to me that I was not the one who put him there, and I would not be the one to remove him. At that moment, the Lord said to me, "Anyone that speaks against my anointed, no matter what their sins are, you are to rebuke them." He charged me to look at the life of David in 1 Samuel 26:7-9:

"So David and Abishai came to the people by night; and there Saul lay sleeping within the camp, with his spear stuck in the ground by his head. Abner and the people lay all around him. Then Abishai said to David, God has delivered your enemy into your hand this day. Now therefore, please, let me strike him at once with the spear, right to the earth; and I will not have to strike him a second time!

But David said to Abishai, Do not destroy him; for who can stretch out his hand against the Lord anointed, and be guiltless?"

These scripture tore me apart; I had been wrong, and I was ashamed about it. With tears in my eyes, I lifted my voice to the Lord and asked what I was to do. He said to me, "You must learn how to walk in the Spirit. If you are in the Spirit, nothing that he can say or do can come near you. Here, you will learn how to guard your heart and to be sensitive to My Very Presence. I will teach you how to walk before Me and My people." I was left humbled and in awe and commanded by the Lord to go back to my church and to apologize for my actions. I was humble and silent for months. I sat in our youth service for two months crying and broken.

In August, our church revival came around, and I went looking to hear from the Lord. The Man of God that night was awesome, and the Spirit of the Lord was wonderful in that place. The man of God began to lay hands and people began to fall under the power of the Spirit. I, however, sat on the third pew broken and sad. The man of God walked out of the church, and our Senior Pastor was left standing alone. He grabbed the microphone and looked straight towards the back of the sanctuary; it was then that he came out of the pulpit to me and said these words: "The Lord has spoken to me and has said it is time for you to come out of the wilderness." I was shocked and amazed, for the Lord had found favor with me. On October 10, 1998, I was licensed as a Minister of the Gospel, and the Youth Pastor who had tried to hinder me did not know about it until two days before the actual event. He himself was left in awe that the Lord had chosen me, but that would not stop the persecution from coming.

Walking in the Spirit

The Lord had to teach me to walk before His people without being drawn into the realms of the flesh by the people. It was obvious that I did not know how to walk before people without reacting to the things people said about me or did to me. I had to learn to lean on the Lord, and that was hard for me. The Lord spoke to me from Galatians 5:16-18:

"I say then: Walk in the Spirit, and you shall not fulfill the lust of the flesh. For the flesh lusts against the Spirit, and the Spirit against the flesh; and these are contrary to one another, so that you do not do the things that you wish. But if you are led by the spirit, you are not under the law."

I had to learn the difference between the flesh and the Spirit. And oh, how the Lord quickly taught me! I would learn how to spend countless hours in prayer, learning how to move by the Spirit of God and the sensitivity of it. My character would become the center point of God's hands, and I would learn how to settle myself in the hands of the Spirit. The months became long for me as I would wrestle with the depth of my flesh, but the end of the process would be good for those who would partake of that which the Lord would have me to go through. I was broken before the Lord, yet my being had been filled with the power of the Spirit. I had learned that the Spirit would be the only way I could live before his people, and that Jesus was the only person God wanted them to see.

The Heart of a Pastor

This new found revelation of the Spirit had pushed me to new heights and new depths. I had received understanding on what I was to become, and what I was not to be like. I had become faithful to my youth ministry, and I went after it with my whole heart. The Sunday had come for me to get the sanctuary in order and to prepare for youth church. I had gotten to the youth church early to set up, and the Youth Pastor was there. As he walked past me, he stopped at the door of the sanctuary. The Holy Spirit had grabbed a hold of him, and he began to prophesy these words to me, "The Spirit of the Lord says that you have the heart of a shepherd, and you will pastor My people." I was left stunned. I did not know what was going on. This was the same man who did not want to see me advance in ministry. Yet the Lord had grabbed a hold of his spirit and led him to release a word over my life which would lead me to the next level of my ministry.

The Power of the Spirit

My ministry had taken off because of my obedience to walk in the Spirit. I started to experience things in the Spirit that I had never experienced before. The prophetic on my life was heavy, and the ministry of healing and deliverance was awesome. I had been at a church in my local city, and the power of the Spirit was on me in great and powerful magnitude. As the Holy Spirit came down to minister to the young people, a demon manifested itself over in the corner of the church. At that moment, a father had come down to me in tears. He said to me, "My wife is in the hospital and has been diagnosed with breast cancer and is due to go into surgery tomorrow; can you please pray for her? Also, my son has kidney problems, and has been on these medications for over six months." I prayed for the mother and son that day and left that youth meeting with the fire of God in my Spirit. Six months had passed, and I was holding a youth revival at my church. A woman came up to me and asked if I knew Keean Sutton. I said, "I am he." She grabbed me and gave me the biggest hug. She said, "I am the woman you prayed for six months ago. I want you to know that when they were preparing me for surgery, the doctor looked at the x-ray and could not find the cancer." Not only that, but her son had not been on his medication ever since the meeting. He had not needed his medication anymore! I was thrilled. At that moment the Lord said to me, "I am confirming your ministry with these signs and wonders; know that I have chosen you." All was well, so I thought.

You Must Leave the Church

All started to go well in the youth ministry at my church, but the Lord saw a bigger picture. I had been preaching so much to the young people at our church that they started to bring their friends. The youth ministry was growing. Please understand that I do not attribute the growth to my work or for my merit. I believe that it grew because of the Holy Spirit and the hard work of all the leaders in the ministry. Yet the Lord visited me and told me to start a ministry outside of my local church. I started this ministry, but I did not know what the Lord had wanted me to call it. Its name would fall into my lap as a couple of friends and I was riding to church. The Lord told me to get the dictionary from the floor of the car. He said to open it, and the word "vigor" stood out at me. "Your ministry will be an active force and strength, bringing victory to young people in My Name: "Vigor" (Victory in God our Redeemer)."

"Wow!" I said, "This is awesome!" I began to put the vision and mission statement together and incorporated the ministry. I was told to hold meetings on the weekends and then training classes for young people who wanted to do ministry to its fullness. On the weekend I opened up, I had a hundred young people. They were excited about what was happening, and we were amazed at the turn out. Now God was going to do great things before our eyes, and we knew it. The word had gotten out about my ministry especially to the leaders of my church. The Youth Pastor was upset and said that I had started a cult. He blasted me in front of all the parents and young people. I was broken, yet I stayed silent and went to the Lord. A meeting was set up for me to come and to talk to the Assistant Pastor of the church. On my way to the meeting, I prayed to the Lord for wisdom and understanding, and He would truly give it. The Assistant Pastor invited me in to his office and said to me these words, "Zeal without understanding leads to nothing." My heart had been captivated by those words. He said to me, "Son, what you are doing is a great thing, but get understanding. Be careful about your ministry and watch out." The Assistant Pastor had approved my ministry that day, and no matter what the Youth Pastor had said, he saw the favor of God on it. Months had passed, and I was called into a meeting with the Senior Pastor of our church. Our meeting place would be in the break room of the church. He asked me what the Lord was calling me to do. I told him, "To minister to young people." With his hands full of grease because of the fish he was eating, He laid hands on me and released me to do my ministry. I was excited that the Lord had given me favor with men, and ministry for me would not be the same as it was for me at my home church.

The young people had scattered because of what the Youth Pastor had done. I was left with one young person, but I was faithful with that young person. I began to develop my ministry, writing down what the Lord had shown me concerning the destiny of Vigor Youth Ministries and the prophetic mantle that would rest on it. The time had come for me to leave my home church. I was fearful because of the concerns that I had for the young people who remained there. Would I be leaving them there to die? My heart had dropped. The Lord said to me, "If you do not go, then this ministry will never become what I want it to be." I left the ministry, yet a great number of young people would be attached to what the Lord was doing. They had decided that where ever I went, they would follow. That day, I was given some of the most amazing young people of my life. Vigor Youth Ministries had finally been birthed.

A Friend's Heart

There were some young people in my ministry from Africa. These young people's hearts had been set ablaze by the glory of the Lord. They were passionate about bringing other young people to our new found ministry. These young people brought a young man who I was proud to call a spiritual son. I began to pour into this young man everything the Lord had placed inside of me. As a spiritual father, it was my duty to do this. I had pulled many young people close to me to give them the prophetic word that was in my belly, and I was excited about the chance to give them the things the Lord had revealed to me concerning them. These young people moved in with me, and our nights would be late as I would impart the Word of the Lord inside of them and teach them how to pray. The Lord had told me to pull these young people close to me to deal with their character, but I did not know what was in store for me when I did this. I had to cut deep, so deep that at the end of our impartation sessions, there would be a long silence and tears. I had to answer the question of whether or not these young people were ready to do what the Lord was calling them to do. The next few months would answer that question. The young man who was brought to me was a young person that had been sheltered, not because there was something wrong with him, but because his mother did not want her child to go through the things that she had gone through. It was hard getting into this kid's house, but I knew that the Lord had brought him to me for a reason. As I imparted into him, the words that fell inside his spirit would catch on fire, and he would go home and spread this word to his family. Soon, the closed door to his home would become an open door. Before we knew it, his mother, brother, and sister would accept Jesus. The mother began to trust me, and she began coming to my services while the Lord won her heart. I had become a father to her son, and I would begin to teach him the basic things in life that a father would teach a son. She would allow him to move in with me, and there I would take him through the process of becoming who God had called him to be. The question I was left with was would he be ready?

A Son's Character Exposed

I was driving down the street with my new son, and I leaned over to him and asked him, "Are you ready for this?" I said to him that this would be a hard move and a life changing one. I shared with him the value of his becoming a man of God and the good things that God wanted to do through him. He told me that day he was ready. Like many young people and adults, he never counted the cost of what the Lord was trying to take him through to get him ready to be a part of the Lord's Army. He would move in with me the summer of 2001, and I opened up my life and my prophetic chambers to him. It was in these chambers that the Lord would begin to expose his character. The nights that we would stay up and discuss his life and ministry became nights of war and turmoil as the Lord pressed me to press his spirit until Christ was formed in him. This young man was a good young man, but he lacked integrity, and I would soon find out the depth of that lack. The spirit of rejection became obvious in his life as he sought the attention and glamour of ministry instead of the humility of the cross. The Lord was very adamant about not raising up another generation who would compromise the integrity of the Gospel and Kingdom to live in the entertainment shadow of the world. His life had become an open box for lust and greed, and now, I was present to deal with that. My words to him about his life and destiny would become words that would fall on a cold heart. He stopped listening, and it was here that he would become the Son of Perdition.

The Son of Perdition

Perdition was the word released from Heaven. The Lord was pressing my spirit to look and to understand that which was going on around me. I had come to a place of denial. I could not believe that the son whom I had come to love would be the one that would allow himself to be subject to the tactics of the enemy. "No, Lord," I said. My heart had become heavy, and my nights had become full of deeply intense prayer. My spirit would not let up; I had to look deep; I had to pay attention to the things that were going on around me; for the Lord was speaking, and my spiritual son would become a sign for a generation that had found themselves in the church for years but had not become mature in their spirits. What is the word *perdition*? The word perdition is the Greek word "Apoleia" which means ruin or destruction. The word of the Lord was very clear to me; He spoke:

"While I was with them in the world, I kept them in thy name: those that thou gavest me I have kept, and none of them is lost, but the son of perdition; that the scripture might be fulfilled" (John 17:12).

What the Lord was saying to me was that the son that I had was allowing his spirit to become ruined. Yet the Word of the Lord would be fulfilled concerning him. I watched this young man get caught up in some of the wildest things. My words had become words of rage to him, and he could no longer take what I was telling him. He began to manipulate to gain his way in life. The scripture had become his main interest of power. Like Satan, he would use these words to become his source of lust and gain. His countenance had changed, and the lives of many would be affected by this change. For the son whom I once knew had now become the son of Perdition--the son of ruin.

The Great Falling Away
"Let no man deceive you by any means: for that day shall not come, except there come a falling away first, and that man of sin be revealed, the son of perdition;" (2Th 2:3).

Two years passed, and it was obvious that my spiritual son's spirit had been ruined. His character had become dark, and his motives were getting more and more cunning--so much so that many of the young people inside my ministry began to be affected by it. He would look for people to affirm his rebellion only to find himself searching for those people outside in the world. The Spirit of the Lord would come to me in 2003 and say that a falling away was coming to my ministry, and many would be affected by the spirit of Judas and be led down a path of destruction. He went on to say, "I want you to know this because this is going on now in My Church. There is a generation that has been affected by the rebellion of leaders who will not submit themselves to the authority that I have put in place in the earth realm. They have become backbiters, gossipers, and rebellious people who do not know the real meaning of submission." My generation had been affected by this false example and false image. "You must teach them the value of authority and the cost for the mantle that they must carry. Go now! And I will be with you says the spirit of God."

Like Jesus, I found myself at the table saying, "One of you will betray me!" And before I knew it, in one week, my spiritual son would turn my ministry into a circus of clowns and foolish young people who only saw themselves and not the God they served and the people they were called to. Several of my young people became filled with pride, stubbornness, and rebellion, and their ears became closed to what the Lord had mandated them to do. With this spirit being birthed in this generation, it was now pushing us closer to the great falling away and the true Son of Perdition. Would a generation of young people be able to stand in the hour of temptation? Would they be able to stand against the schemes of the devil or fall into his evil traps? I would find out because little did I know there was evil brewing against me, and it was coming from the South. My faith would be tested; who I was as a man of God would be put on display. And the ministry that the Lord had given me would take on the biggest challenge of its life.

My life had become broken, and my knees were as feeble as a horse whose legs have just been broken. The Spirit of Judas was out to do damage, but it would take the Spirit of Christ to defeat it. If the generation that is now at hand is going to survive, then, that generation must become more than another song or class act. It must take upon the role of a yielded vessel ready to leave a mark for Jesus and to suffer for His name's sake. Could that generation be out there? Could that generation be the one that would stand against the spirit of Judas, or would it become another victim of Judas itself?

CHAPTER 8

THE SPIRIT OF JEZEBEL

"In the thirty-eighth year of Asa king of Judah, Ahab son of Omri became king of Israel, and he reigned in Samaria over Israel twenty-two years. Ahab son of Omri did more evil in the eyes of the Lord than any of those before him. He not only considered it trivial to commit the sins of Jeroboam son of Nebat, but he also married Jezebel daughter of Ethbaal king of the Sidonians, and began to serve Baal and worship him" (1Kings 16:29-31).

It was the year of 2003; my son had betrayed me, and my heart was full of pain and hurt. My wife and I had been going through some changes that had really pushed me to the limits. I was frustrated, angry, and hurt. My mind had been playing tricks on me, and no one around me knew how hurt I was. Like many young people, silent pain can become dangerous especially if not dealt with. I lay down in the bed one night, and the Lord put me in a deep sleep. I saw the spirit of Jezebel trying to get me. This is the first time in my life that I am talking about what the Lord showed me that night. I have been silent until now. No one knew what I had seen, not even my wife. I ignored the dream as it had become dumb to me, and I did not believe it was true. My unbelief would cost me. I was punished seven years and put out of several realms of the Lord's mind of which I had access. I was hurt, lost, and lonely. I was kicked out of His mind, and I missed how being in the Lord's mind brought great truth and revelation. I did not understand that which had befallen me, and if I had renewed my mind, then, I would not have lost the Mind of Christ. I took a breath, for I was getting ready to go on a long journey.

A Culture Birthed

Several years had passed, and the Lord spoke to me again about the spirit of Jezebel. He told me to get ready for it, for she was trying to spread her father's culture. In the chapter, "Annihilation of the Seed," I talked to you about the word culture and what it meant (see Chapter 2). Here in 1 Kings 16, you see that Jezebel's father sticks out like a sore thumb. The Lord has always been trying to expose Jezebel, but the church has looked at her only as a spirit and not one assigned to bring forth a wicked culture. Ethbaal's (Jezebel's father) name means "with him is Baal." Baal's name means "Master or Lord." Ethbaal ruled over the cities of Sidon and Tyre. In Ezekiel 28:1-19, God speaks to Ezekiel about the pride of the King of Tyre and his haughty heart; he said:

"The word of the Lord came to me: 'Son of man, say to the ruler of Tyre, 'This is what the Sovereign Lord says: 'In the pride of your heart you say, "I am a god; I sit on the throne of a god in the heart of the seas.' But you are a man and not a god, though you think you are as wise as a god. Are you wiser than Daniel? Is no secret hidden from you? By your wisdom and understanding you have gained wealth for yourself and amassed gold and silver in your treasuries. By your great skill in trading you have increased

your wealth, and because of your wealth your heart has grown proud. Therefore this is what the Sovereign Lord says: 'Because you think you are wise, as wise as a god, I am going to bring foreigners against you, the most ruthless of nations; they will draw their swords against your beauty and wisdom and pierce your shining splendor. They will bring you down to the pit, and you will die a violent death in the heart of the seas. Will you then say, 'I am a god,' in the presence of those who kill you? You will be but a man, not a god, in the hands of those who slay you. You will die the death of the uncircumcised at the hands of foreigners. I have spoken, declares the Sovereign Lord.'"

The Word of the Lord came to me: "Son of man, take up a lament concerning the king of Tyre and say to him: 'This is what the Sovereign Lord says: "'You were the model of perfection, full of wisdom and perfect in beauty. You were in Eden, the garden of God; every precious stone adorned you: ruby, topaz and emerald, chrysolite, onyx and jasper, sapphire, turquoise and beryl. Your settings and mountings were made of gold; on the day you were created they were prepared. You were anointed as a guardian cherub, for so I ordained you. You were on the holy mount of God; you walked among the fiery stones. You were blameless in your ways from the day you were created till wickedness was found in you. Through your widespread trade you were filled with violence, and you sinned. So I drove you in disgrace from the

mount of God, and I expelled you, O guardian cherub, from among the fiery stones. Your heart became proud on account of your beauty, and you corrupted your wisdom because of your splendor. So I threw you to the earth; I made a spectacle of you before kings. By your many sins and dishonest trade you have desecrated your sanctuaries. So I made a fire come out from you, and it consumed you, and I reduced you to ashes on the ground in the sight of all who were watching. All the nations who knew you are appalled at you; you have come to a horrible end and will be no more.'"

Ethbaal had considered himself to be a god. His purpose was to spread Baalism throughout the entire world. Here, Baal would have lordship over the world, but in order for him to do so, he would have to overthrow the greatest kingdom of the world, "Israel." Ethbaal had come up with a plan that would allow his plan to come forth and for Baal to be glorified in the earth. The Spirit of the Lord was clear to me about this fact. Satan is trying to rule the earth, and he needs to get to a generation to do it. He will use the simplest thing in the earth to do it, but it will do great damage to a generation as it has in the past destroyed many generations. I asked, "What would this simple thing be, Lord?" His response to me would be "Authority." The Greek word for "Authority" is delegated influence with jurisdiction, liberty, power, right, and strength. Ethbaal wanted more influence. He wanted more jurisdiction, liberty, power, might, and strength. He wanted to control a culture, a people, a nation. But in order for him to do this, he needed to capture an authority that had been delegated. The word *delegate* means to entrust to another, to appoint, to pass down. With this authority being delegated, it says that it is authentic. It's real, and everyone looks to it for answers. God had established Israel as the number one voice in the earth. It was through Israel that God would teach all the nations of the earth how to worship and come into who they really were in the earth. The meaning of Israel's name is "Prince." *Prince* means leader, initiator, and king. Ethbaal, knowing that Israel was such a great leader, devised a plan to take out King Ahab, the leader of Israel. Ahab had been a young man when he became king of Israel and was very passive and naive about the things of God. He had learned his tactics and ways from his father, King Omri, who taught him not the ways of God. So when time came for Ahab to be married, he would join in his father's covenant relationship with Ethbaal and marry his daughter Jezebel. Jezebel's name means "where is the prince" or where is the leader, initiator, or king. Jezebel had to do four things:

1. Capture the heart of the King
2. Have a son by that King
3. Capture the culture of Israel
4. Establish Baal as Lord and Master

The Lord had hit me with a blow that I was not ready for. Our generation has fallen into something deep, something so severe that if we don't wake up and catch this, we will be doomed. Satan is trying to capture a holy culture that is beyond his reach. Yet there is a generation that is at hand that is getting ready to receive a mantle passed down to them from our forefathers. However, our generation has fallen into the tricks and trade of the enemy. We have compromised so much to fit in that the things God has called holy have become common. Many of our forefathers have taught us that it is acceptable to live two separate lives and to dishonor and discredit the established authority that has been in the earth. This is because many of our forefathers did not like what many of their fathers were saying to them and getting them ready for. For them, it had to be on their terms or no terms at all. So a generation arose with the doctrine of "you don't need man as long as you have access to God." This teaching has gotten us in trouble. Yes, we have access to God through Jesus Christ, but Jesus never threw out established authority in the earth. The purpose for this authority was for us as a people and generation to become disciplined in the things of God and to be ready to take upon a mantle set for us by the fathers of the faith He has given us. Yet the liberty that the Lord has given us through the shedding of His blood has been misused as a means of sin and not righteousness.

Jezebel needed to knock out our God by taking over the leadership that had the influence over the culture that God had given that leader. She had to get that leader to see that the authority that he knew and the value of the people's God was not real nor was it authentic. If she could get the leader to see this, then the leader's authority would be dismantled, and his mind would be an open door for control. Youth ministries are falling all over the place especially in the Black church. I know many black pastors may not want to hear this, but the truth is that we have not developed our young people in the church to handle the ministries that have been given to us. We have used entertainment as a means of keeping our young people excited about church, yet the character of our young people is the same as it was when they came in. This is not the case for all black churches. Some have caught the mandate which the Lord has given us for our generation, but many have used youth ministry as a career move in ministry and a place where they can exert their own authority. Many Senior Pastors have made the move of just putting anyone over their youth ministry and those who have been ordained by God to train the next generation for leadership have been overlooked or even dismissed from the church. So by the time the young person becomes a senior in high school, s/he goes off to college only to get caught up in the realms of the flesh and taunted by the cares of this world. Youth ministry for the Lord has always been a place where young people can come to find out who they are and what the Lord is calling them to do. It is in those places that young people find destiny and go on to do great exploits for the Lord. Unfortunately, the spirit of Jezebel has captured the hearts of many of these men and women of God who say they are called to youth ministry, and because they don't know what to do with the young people they have, they have opened a door where Jezebel can come in and dictate the outcome and purpose of a generation. So now, the culture that was once outside our youth ministry, in the world, has become a youth ministry that looks like the world and smells just like the world, leaving no one around the church, not even the Senior Pastor, able to tell the difference.

Like Ethbaal, we have presented Jezebel to our young people and told them to marry her. Now, she has control over a generation. She knows that they are the ones to carry the mantle. She knows that they are the ones to prepare the way for the second coming. The problem is that we don't know!

The State of Rebellion

It was April of 2008, and I was sent to Utica, New York by the Lord to declare one of the hardest words of my life. The Word of the Lord was in my mouth, and I knew that what the Lord was saying to me would change the outlook of a generation and separate the wheat from the tare. I knew that not all the young people in this generation would stand up and answer the Divine Call of God on their lives, but the Lord was clear about what he was getting ready to do. This one declaration in the atmosphere would begin to separate the seed of God and the seed of Satan. The world was getting ready to change. Our country was getting ready to put into office our first black president, and whenever there is a change in leadership, according to scripture, God always begins to raise up a prophet that he has had in training for a season. It was clear that God was getting ready to raise up His generation, but He had to weed them out from the rest of those that were at the place of rebellion. God began to speak to me from Ezekiel 2:3-8:

"He said: Son of man, I am sending you to the Israelities, to a rebellious nation that has rebelled against me; they and their fathers have been in revolt against me this very day. The people to whom I am sending you are obstinate and stubborn. Say to them, "This is what the sovereign Lord says. And whether they listen or fail to listen, for they are a rebellious house – they will know that a prophet has been among them And you, son of man do not be afraid, though briers and thorns are all around you and you live among scorpions. Do not be afraid of what they say or terrified by them though they are a rebellious house. You must speak my words to them whether they listen or fail to listen, for they are a rebellious. But you, son son of man, listen to what I say to you. Do not rebel like that rebellious house; open your mouth and eat what I give you."

This word was very deep in my spirit, and I struggled with it. My spirit was in turmoil, and my heart was fainting, for I knew the opposition that I would face concerning this. I knew that it would not start with those outside the church, but it would start with those inside our local youth churches. My ministry would be the first example of God ridding rebellion from the earth as I began to deal with the spirit of Jezebel.

Who knew that they were operating under the spirit of Jezebel? Many were blinded by their actions and deeds under the covenant where God had placed me. I knew the people; I could see this spirit working hard in their lives, and I knew how far to go with them. The evil spirit of Jezebel did not want me to deal with her. She looked for ways of trapping me into her ways. She looked for things to say and to do, and I must admit that I almost lost focus on the target at hand, but the Lord reminded me of my charge and that I must keep it. I was deep in sorrow, for her spirit was strong on my ministry. She began to attack my sons and daughters, and they were unaware of her tactics. One by one, she would trick each of them to form an alliance with her drawing them all close to the brink of rebellion. She taught them her ways, for they all had become her students, and each one of them would raise their hands every time she asked a question. "Who are these people?" I thought, for this is not the ministry that the Lord had given me. We were born to be children of valor, those who lived in deep communion with the Lord. My cry was for His presence; my heart wanted nothing more than for my ministry to please Him and Him alone. "What are you showing me, Lord? I cannot take this; did I open this door? Did I cause this rebellion?

I began to search my heart, yet I would be placed in a position where my eyes would see more rebellion. Those who were close to me could not stand. A young lady had been very close to my heart as I was sent to her life to teach her the value of being a woman of God. She had to learn that character was important if she was to carry the mantle of intercession on her life. She went backward and forward with the spirit of rebellion wanting more from the world than that of God. She had the means to touch the heart of God through her worship, but Jezebel's call was too much for her to handle. She had submitted to Jezebel's truths, her values, her ways of life. She did not understand that she could not have what she wanted; she did not know that what she wanted was not what God wanted for her, so she chose Jezebel to be her partner, her lover for life. She was eager and passionate not to follow authority. She wanted to cripple it; she wanted to see all those who were in authority hurt. This was because her life was not what she wanted it to be.

Like many young people in the world today, we have taken the pain in our lives and used it as a means to sin. This young lady did not want me to say anything to her about her life. Her life was messy, and I was the cause of it. Jezebel looks to kill the Voice of God's Prophet. This is because the prophet is the Voice of a Generation, a culture, a people. The prophet is to give insight to the generation, that culture, that people, and lead them to a place of repentance and understanding. His or her purpose is to lead the people to the heart of God and to deal with the warfare that would stop a people, generation, and culture from getting to the Living God. That is why God was pushing me to train a generation to deal with the demonic forces of Jezebel. I cannot tell you all how important it is to be ready for the Lord's Call. We must be ready to deal with the spirit that is trying to kill the mantle over our lives. We must fight for our culture, our generation, and our people.

The Lord told me, "This is why I have shown you this, and this is why I have called you." Remember what is written in the Book of Revelation 2:20-29:

"Nevertheless, I have this against you: You tolerate that woman Jezebel, who calls herself a prophetess. By her teaching she misleads my servants into sexual immorality and the eating of food sacrificed to idols.
I have given her time to repent of her immorality, but she is unwilling. So I will cast her on a bed of suffering, and I will make those who commit adultery with her suffer intensely, unless they repent of her ways. I will strike her children dead. Then all the churches will know that I am he who searches hearts and minds, and I will repay each of you according to your deeds. Now I say to the rest of you in Thyatira, to you who do not hold to her teaching and have not learned Satan's so-called deep secrets (I will not impose any other burden on you): Only hold on to what you have until I come. To him who overcomes and does my will to the end, I will give authority over the nations-- 'He will rule them with an iron scepter; he will dash them to pieces like pottery'-- just as I have received authority from my Father. I will also give him the morning star. He, who has an ear, let him hear what the Spirit says to the churches."

CHAPTER 9
THE INIQUITY OF THE SANCTUARY

"The Lord said to Aaron, 'You, your sons and your father's family are to bear the responsibility for offenses against the sanctuary, and you and your sons alone are to bear the responsibility for offenses against the priesthood. Bring your fellow Levites from your ancestral tribe to join you and assist you when you and your sons minister before the Tent of the Testimony. They are to be responsible to you and are to perform all the duties of the Tent, but they must not go near the furnishings of the sanctuary or the altar, or both they and you will die. They are to join you and be responsible for the care of the Tent of Meeting--all the work at the Tent--and no one else may come near where you are. You are to be responsible for the care of the sanctuary and the altar, so that wrath will not fall on the Israelites again. I myself have selected your fellow Levites from among the Israelites as a gift to you, dedicated to the Lord to do the work at the Tent of Meeting. But only you and your sons may serve as priests in connection with everything at the altar and inside the curtain. I am giving you the service of the priesthood as a gift. Anyone else who comes near the sanctuary must be put to death.'"

A Holy Priesthood was what God wanted from this generation, not a priesthood of the old Covenant nor that which many of our forefathers had developed, but that of the Priesthood of Christ. The

Lord was very clear when He spoke this word to me. "I am developing this generation after the order of Christ's Priesthood." Now remember what I told you in the chapter "The Rise of the Priesthood." Priests are those that engage in Holy Matters. If this is so, then our generation has entered into a serious amount of trouble, and we have been left with something for which we refuse to take responsibility. That is the care of the house of God.

We know that the Lord is not trapped by the four walls of a building, but do we understand that what we have committed to the Lord is His to keep and use as His dwelling place. The Lord has put us as a generation in charge of one of the most precious things ever, and that is His presence, but we have allowed things to come in that the Lord had never intended. Our youth ministries are filled with entertainment, and lost young people who have no vision or purpose. This has left God's house undone, and many of the young people inside our youth ministries are surviving off the entertainment bug and not the presence of God. This goes for all churches whether Black, White, Asian, or Hispanic: all have been hit with the entertainment bug. We as youth pastors have not taught you as young people your roles inside the church and have not given you your correct responsibility regarding the sanctuary of the Lord. This is a dangerous spot for any youth ministry to be in. Without the proper teaching, anything can come into a youth ministry and cause great damage. As well, young people can come in and have no reverence for the house of the Lord, and if that is so, they will have no reverence for the presence of God.

The Damage of the Sons of Eli

'Eli's sons were wicked men; they had no regard for the Lord. Now it was the practice of the priests with the people that whenever anyone offered a sacrifice and while the meat was being boiled, the servant of the priest would come with a three-pronged fork in his hand. He would plunge it into the pan or kettle or caldron or pot, and the priest would take for himself whatever the fork brought up. This is how they treated all the Israelites who came to Shiloh. But even before the fat was burned, the servant of the priest would come and say to the man who was sacrificing, 'Give the priest some meat to roast; he won't accept boiled meat from you, but only raw.'' If the man said to him, 'Let the fat be burned up first, and then take whatever you want,' the servant would then answer, 'No, hand it over now; if you don't, I'll take it by force.' This sin of the young men was very great in the Lord's sight, for they were treating the Lord's offering with contempt" (1 Samuel 2:12-17).**

The sons of Eli had become wicked in their dealings with that which belong to the Lord. They had no respect or regard for that which the Lord was trying to do for His people. Like Eli's sons, most of the young people today have no respect for the Lord's house. They have no regard for those things which are holy. This disregard of holy things is due to a lack of teaching on the part of those that God has called to teach a generation about those things which are holy. Unlike Eli's sons, I can truly say that eighty per cent of our youth leaders today have not been taught about handling the Lord's presence with care. Therefore, they are unable to teach a generation about handling the Lord's presence with care. This disrespect causes major trouble in Heaven, for the Lord was not pleased with that which Eli sons had been doing.

"Now a man of God came to Eli and said to him, 'This is what the Lord says: 'Did I not clearly reveal myself to your father's house when they were in Egypt under Pharaoh? I chose your father out of all the tribes of Israel to be my priest, to go up to my altar, to burn incense, and to wear an ephod in my presence. I also gave your father's house all the offerings made with fire by the Israelites. Why do you scorn my sacrifice and offering that I prescribed for my dwelling? Why do you honor your sons more than me by fattening yourselves on the choice parts of every offering made by my people Israel?' "Therefore the Lord, the God of Israel, declares: 'I promised that your house and your father's house would minister before me forever.' But now the Lord declares: 'Far be it from me! Those who honor me I will honor, but those who despise me will be disdained. The time is coming when I will cut short your strength and the strength of your

father's house, so that there will not be an old man in your family line and you will see distress in my dwelling. Although good will be done to Israel, in your family line there will never be an old man. Every one of you that I do not cut off from my altar will be spared only to blind your eyes with tears and to grieve your heart, and all your descendants will die in the prime of life. '"And what happens to your two sons, Hophni and Phinehas, will be a sign to you--they will both die on the same day" (1Samuel 2:27-34).

The death of a generation is due to our lack of teaching them the importance of the presence of God. I learned this early in my ministry, as I was instructed by the Lord to guard His presence with all my heart and soul. I was to teach the young people in my ministry the sensitivity of the presence of God and how the small things would grieve Him if we are not careful. I had to teach a generation the same respect if I was to prepare them to carry the presence of God to the nations. My heart has ached for many youth ministries that I see that are on the chopping block. Young people are losing their spiritual and physical lives due to lack of sincerity, honor, and reverence of that which belongs to the Lord. God never intended for this generation to get lost in the ignorance of learning how to approach Him in His house. They had to learn how to pray, worship, sing, and dance. They had to learn how to properly release the Word of the Spirit to those that are in need and how to minister to a dying people. People are supposed to find healing and restoration in the House of the Lord. Yet a generation has risen that only sees God's House as a means of comfort and and relief from boredom. Our generation does not even work hard to keep the House of the Lord organized and clean. They have been taught to have their hands out for everything. They say in their hearts, "I will do this if you give me this." Or "if they are not paying me, I am not doing anything." These things have offended God and have brought sin to the very place where His presence is supposed to dwell, yet no young person, youth leader, or youth pastor will stand up and say anything about it. Eli enjoyed the sins of his sons, and he never said anything to them. For the Lord, that in itself brought reproach to His presence. For any leader not to speak up when the presence of God is being disrespected because of immaturity is a dishonor to the Lord and the house where His name abides.

The Building of an Image

There is a personality that comes with every young person, and if every young person carries personality, then every youth ministry carries a personality. If this is so, then what is the personality of our generation? We have been called to guard the very presence of God. With that comes a responsibility that most young people are not ready to pay. Captivated by the world, most young people who are inside our local youth ministries have a hard time letting the world go. With so much pressure from the world system, young people's hearts become filled with uncertainty and misdirection, and with all of this going on in their hearts, young people have become filled with emotions that

104

begin to creep inside our youth ministries. When this happens, young people begin to ask for an image that they themselves are not ready to take on. In Exodus 32:2-5:

"So Aaron said, 'Take the gold rings from the ears of your wives and sons and daughters, and bring them to me.' All the people took the gold rings from their ears and brought them Aaron. Then Aaron took the gold, melted it down, and molded it into the shape of a calf. When the people saw it, they exclaimed, 'O Israel, these are the gods who brought you out of the land of Egypt!' Aaron saw how excited the people were, so he built an altar in front of the calf. Then he announced, "Tomorrow will be festival to the Lord!"

Today's youth pastors have compromised the integrity of the Word of the Lord as well as the presence of God trying to relate to young people. The Lord was very clear to me concerning this generation. His words to me were, "Do not compromise the integrity of My presence trying to reach young people; allow my presence to captivate them. They will come. My image is very important, and nothing shall get in the way of that." I have understood the temptation of wanting to see young people drawn to the Lord by giving them programs and entertainment that do not feed their spirits or challenge them to go higher. We have gotten caught up trying to use the world's means to draw and keep our young people inside our ministries. This kind of compromise does not help the young person see who God is. This only causes future trouble for the youth ministry and the young person. Aaron's issue was that he did not have the courage to stand up for the Lord's image. Aaron was not willing to protect the Lord's presence. He took what the people were wearing and developed for them what they wanted. When the people saw what Aaron had given them they got excited. We have made images for young people that have tickled their bones and made them feel like the world. Yet fifty percent of the young people inside our local ministry can barely quote the basic scriptures. Nor do they have a prayer life beyond saying "thank you Jesus." The Lord has been floored by the disrespect of that which our youth leaders have come up with, and with the turn of the century, a generation is not prepared to take on the mantle of that which has been left for them. I want all to know that are reading this book that I am not against Holy Hip Hop, Rock, or any other forms of worship. I know that it is from the Lord. But when secular music has filled our sanctuary or rock music that sounds like it has come from the heart of the band KISS, then there are some serious problems going on. The Lord has released a spirit of creativity in the earth for every Youth Pastor to tap into; it comes with the anointing of the Youth Pastor. When this anointing has been tapped into, then young people will walk into that creativity, and the gifts inside of them will begin to flourish. We must be careful that we don't give young people the very thing that they have been called out of (the World). Image for a young person is everything, and if you give them an image that they were never created in, then they will began to produce the fruit of that image and draw other young people to the fruit of that image. Remember what God said in Genesis 1:26: "Then God said, "Let us make man in our image, in our likeness.""

Image for God is everything, and when we produce an image that He never created us to walk in, then we will find ourselves like Aaron. God was clear to me when He spoke about this deception, and even now, I hear Him saying to me, "Destroy the images that they have built."

The Destruction of an Image

The Lord had brought to my attention the Image that has been set up in our generation, and my assignment was to completely destroy that image. This was going to take boldness, for not everyone was ready to stand up to this image. The Lord knew and wanted me to know that there was going to be a split in a generation, and it was going to come from the young people inside of the generation that were willing to take a stand and not be with the majority. This meant that those young people had to have the ability to hear the voice of spiritual authority when they said move. In Exodus 32:27-28, you will read these words:

"Then Moses stood in the gate of the camp, and said, Who is on the Lord's side? Let him come unto me. And all the sons of Levi gathered themselves unto him. And he said unto them, Thus saith the Lord God of Israel, Put every man his sword by his side, and go in and out from gate to gate throughout the camp, and slay

every man his brother, and every man his companion, and every man his neighbor.
And the children of Levi did according to the word of Moses: and there fell of the people that day about three thousand men."

If we are to push forth in this hour, in this dispensation, then the image of this dispensation must be destroyed. Youth Pastors and Youth Leaders must understand that a generation is being lost due to what we have set up. The Word of the Lord has said that this image must be destroyed. Right now, God is preparing a generation that will stand up and deal with the image that has been set up. This generation will come with boldness and a sword that will pierce through the heart of this false identity. We as Youth Pastors must stand up and say, "Whoever is on the Lord's side let him come now." Only when this is done will the generation that is called to destroy this image come forth. They are called to destroy over three thousand demonic influences in this generation, and yet we must understand the importance of their coming forth and their being trained to deal with that image. When we have come to this understanding, then we will see this false image destroyed.

CHAPTER 10
THE FOREFATHER'S MANTLE

"And what shall I more say? for the time would fail me to tell of Gideon, and of Barak, and of Samson, and of Jephthah; of David also, and Samuel, and of the prophets: Who through faith subdued kingdoms, wrought righteousness, obtained promises, stopped the mouths of lions, quenched the violence of fire, escaped the edge of the sword, out of weakness were made strong, waxed valiant in fight, turned to flight the armies of the aliens. Women received their dead raised to life again: and others were tortured, not accepting deliverance; that they might obtain a better resurrection: And others had trial of cruel mockings and scourgings, yea, moreover of bonds and imprisonment: They were stoned, they were sawn asunder, were tempted, were slain with the sword: they wandered about in sheepskins and goatskins; being destitute, afflicted, tormented;(Of whom the world was not worthy:) they wandered in deserts, and in mountains, and in dens and caves of the earth. And these all, having obtained a good report through faith, received not the promise: God having provided some better thing for us, that they without us should not be made perfect" (Hebrews 11:32-39).

When the Lord called me into this ministry, I was assigned by the Lord to take a look into the past and see the many men and women of God whom the Lord had used to bring forth His will in the earth. I was astonished as to what I found. I began to read a story about a man by the name of Smith Wigglesworth. This man of God's life changed the way I approached God. He was a man that lived in prayer and in The Word of God. His life changed the hearts of many and brought many to the knowledge of our Lord and Savior Jesus Christ. My eyes filled with tears as I read the amazing stories about this man, and my heart grew with hunger. I was pushed to look up more of these great men and women and came to a woman by the name of Kathryn Kuhlman. From there, I was led to William Seymour, John G. Lake, William Branham, Aimee McPherson, Lester Sumrall, and many more. These men and women of God walked in a power that people only imagine today. I was hungry for what they had and wanted to know how to get it. My quest brought me before God with questions of these great men and women. The Lord would make me understand the truth about these men and women and the mantles which they carried. Trapped in the closets of eternity were mantles, and most of them had been locked up because the people in their generation had become too rebellious and wicked to handle them. Spiritual sons and daughters were not ready to receive the mantles because of their lack of preparation and they did not understand the authority of spiritual Mothers and Fathers in that day. Now a generation has arisen only to have no respect for authority and no reverence for the God who put them there. David understood one thing about King Saul, and that was "He was King." David understood that he could not take a kingdom for himself; it had to be given. If David would have taken the crown before his time, the kingdom would have suffered, and David would have been guilty of killing an anointed King. What was the Lord saying to me? Four things:

1. The fathers of the faith have mantles that are locked up.
2. A generation has taken on the rebellion of their fathers.
3. Am I ready to unlock the Mantles of the Forefathers?
4. They cannot be complete without us.

The Lord wanted me to understand the mystery of this revelation and the importance of me preparing a generation to receive these mantles for the 21st century. Many people will not agree with you. The days of wickedness are ahead, and the spiritual warfare will be stronger than ever before. The unlocking of our forefathers' mantles rests on the backs of a remnant generation being ready to be obedient to the Lord, and they have to understand the depth of these mantle and the enemies that have come along with them.

What I had to do was get the generation to see the importance of entering into a season of preparation. The hard part about all of this was getting them to see the importance of the preparation. The question that lay before me was would they be willing to grind out the tough days of disciplining their emotions and becoming seasoned by the spirit of the Lord? Were they ready to have an old mindset snatched out of them to take upon the mind of the Lord? Were they ready to have their hearts changed and filled with a mission and cause greater than themselves? Were they ready to handle the persecution of their day and fight the wars of their fathers? I saw that this generation is not ready, and no one has taught them how to be ready for it. The burden of the Lord came upon me not because I was perfect and had it all together, but because He saw a generation who was left without teachers, shepherds, prophets, and those who were called to prepare them for the mantles of fathers who had paid a price for them to receive such an honor. I was speechless, for a generation had been called, and our fathers cannot be complete without us.

The Warfare of a Prophet

What this generation does not understand is the price that our forefathers paid in order for them to move under the power of God. Our generation has to know the depth of the call and the ministry which they are called to and the importance of the mantle of the day. The war that our forefathers were under was great, but that war came at a price that allowed us to stand where we stand today. Under the mantle of Elijah, Elisha had to see the warfare that the prophet Elijah was under in order for him to receive his mantle. In 2 kings 2:9-10 you will read:

"And so it was, when they had crossed over, that Elijah said to Elisha, "Ask! What may I do for you before I am taken away from you? Elisha said, "Please let a double portion of your spirit be upon me."

So he said, "You have asked a hard thing, Nevertheless, if you see me when I am taken from you, it shall be so for you; but if not, it shall not be so."

Elisha had to walk where Elijah walked, and if he was to carry Elijah's mantle, he had to understand the enemies that Elijah had to face and deal with those enemies as the Lord saw fit. The young prophet had to follow the man that quickly put his mantle on him to get him to experience the tangible prophetic anointing. The mantle which he experienced was now at the point of being lost to him if he did not understand or see the warfare that he was up under. I have learned that being a prophet is not about how many signs and wonders can be performed through my hands, but the importance of the assignment that is set before me. Our generation has stopped following the men and women of God because they have been taught that they don't need men to get to God, but that they have their own access to Him. I believe that we all have access to the Lord, but God left His kingdom in the Hands of Jesus, and Jesus left it into our hands. With this came a spiritual order that made us as leaders accountable for the souls of those that came under our leadership. What our fathers have taught us has led us to stop following men and women of God who have paid a price for that which is authentic and true--men and women of God who have fought battles to bring forth the kingdom and establish the name of Jesus in the earth. We have accepted this teaching not because it is right, but because it is in the human nature to rebel against the spiritual Law of God. The Lord wanted me to understand this when I sat under a man whose heart was not right towards God. I had to understand authority if I was to receive a mantle. I had to understand the warfare that fathers had to fight in order to receive the mantle that made them sons and daughters who laid down their crowns for something greater than themselves. I had to possess a message for a generation. I was sent to bring back a spiritual law that many would not accept, but many would be willing to pay the price for. I was to unlock the mantle of our forefathers, but I had to see the warfare, and those that followed had to do the same. Elisha followed Elijah through the deep water of the Jordan, and when they came to dry ground, Elijah turned to his young apprentice and said, "Ask! What may I do for you, before I am taken away from you?" Elisha knew right then that what he was going to ask for was going to be great, but he did not know that his eyes would have to grasp the heart of the mantle of which he sought. Elijah looked at him and said, "You have asked a hard thing. Nevertheless, if you see me when I am taken from you, it shall be so for you, but if not, it shall not be so." Everything depended on his ability to see. The Lord pushed me to understand this. Son, can this generation see? Can they see the war that is going on, the battle for God's kingdom, the fight for humanity? Can they see the darkness that is trying to pull us into a deep trench? If they cannot see, then they are not worthy of the mantle which lies before them. Elisha had to see, and before he knew it, the very prophet that he walked with, cried with, shared with, the very man whose hands he had washed, was now being taken away by a chariot of fire and a whirlwind that separated the two of them. And with a cry from the depth of his heart, Elisha saw it. "My father," he exclaimed, "The chariot of Israel and its horsemen!" The Lord sent a chariot of fighting horsemen because the warfare over Elijah's life was great, and Elisha had seen it. With tears in his eyes, the young prophet looked down and saw the mantle of his spiritual father. With great pain and sorrow, the young prophet walked back to the very road that he and his father had traveled. He came to the river where his father had done a miraculous sign. He rolled up the mantle of his father and shouted, "Where is the God of Elijah?" He struck the waters, and the young prophet knew then that he possessed something great.

Shepherds in the Wilderness

The mantle that this generation is to receive has been shaken by sons and daughters who have left their fathers' houses in anger. Most of this has happened because many wanted to be promoted in ministry, or issues of their pastors' teachings fueled a major concern for those that did not agree with the same teachings that the Senior Pastor had taught. Many left because they had been hurt by other members of the church and saw too much wrong among the leadership. The truth is most of our mothers and fathers move before their season and missed a time when God was trying to mature them. With this came anger at the church. Bitterness was born, and now, the church is under great distress within. In all of this, a generation was being born under a cloud of great turmoil. The Lord wanted me to understand the issues that were at hand. He wanted me to look and see what has been created in His Body. God said, "It cannot be so for a generation. Tell them freedom is only given to those who understand the discipline of freedom." They must understand that freedom on the cross was not a means to bypass the Lord's authority or mishandle the grace that was given to His body. But this generation has to understand the value of the authority that was given to help them move into their destiny. They can not be the ones to repeat the sins of the fathers. God wants his young leaders to understand honor, commitment, and loyalty. They have to understand faithfulness. They must have the ability to hear and be shaped into the very image of God. They cannot allow themselves to be moved by immaturity. If this was so, then they would lose the mantles that are locked away for them. They must be patient and learn from those that Lord has put before them. He is not going to send any ordinary leaders: He is going to send leaders that have His heart for them, leaders who have the ability to prepare them for the leadership they will have to walk in for the 21st century. But they will have to be prepared to follow the men and women of God that He has placed in their lives. This simple obedience is going to bring about a Fivefold blessing:

1. It will establish the Law of Spiritual Authority in the earth.
2. It will prepare a generation for their generation.
3. It will prepare a generation to deal with the forefather's enemies as well as demonic influences of the day.

4. It will release the mantle of the forefathers that has been locked up for centuries.

5. It will unlock the mysteries of our generation and help prepare the way for the second coming of the Lord.

Maturity was and is the key for the Lord. A generation had to grow up. They had to understand that they were not going to get everything they wanted. They could not be complainers and people who did not understand the process of ministry. They had to be leaders of vision, integrity, and humility. They had to learn how to be shepherds in the midst of suffering. In Numbers 14:30:34 you will read this:

"Not one of you will enter the land I swore with uplifted hand to make your home, except Caleb son of Jephunneh and Joshua son of Nun. As for your children that you said would be taken as plunder, I will bring them in to enjoy the land you have rejected. But you--your bodies will fall in this desert. Your children will be shepherds here for forty years,] suffering for your unfaithfulness, until the last of your bodies lies in the desert. For forty years--one year for each of the forty days you explored the land--you will suffer for your sins and know what it is like to have me against you."

The young people in this chapter would face the ultimate challenge. They had to face their parents' sin. With this came a promise factor.

They would learn how to be shepherds in the midst of pain. The Lord wanted me to understand this because it was and is key to the generation leading us to the place where the Lord had chosen to put His name. In the wilderness of their parents' doubt, pain, and shame, a generation would learn the meaning of leadership and the importance of being a shepherd.

A Father's Spirit

"Gehazi, the servant of Elisha the man of God, said to himself, "My master was too easy on Naaman, this Aramean, by not accepting from him what he brought. As surely as the LORD lives, I will run after him and get something from him." So Gehazi hurried after Naaman. When Naaman saw him running toward him, he got down from the chariot to meet him. "Is everything all right?" he asked."Everything is all right," Gehazi answered. "My master sent me to say, 'Two young men from the company of the prophets have just come to me from the hill country of Ephraim. Please give them a talent of silver and two sets of clothing." "By all means, take two talents," said Naaman. He urged Gehazi to accept them, and then tied up the two talents of silver in two bags, with two sets of clothing. He gave them to two of his servants, and they carried them ahead of Gehazi. When Gehazi came to the hill, he took the things from the servants and put them away in the house. He sent the men away and they left. Then he went in and stood before his master Elisha. "Where have you

been, Gehazi?" Elisha asked. "Your servant didn't go anywhere,"
Gehazi answered. But Elisha said to him, "Was not my spirit with
you when the man got down from his chariot to meet you? Is this
the time to take money, or to accept clothes, olive groves,
vineyards, flocks, herds, or menservants and maidservants?
Naaman's leprosy will cling to you and to your descendants
forever." Then Gehazi went from Elisha's presence and he was
leprous, as white as snow"
(2 Kings 5:20-27).

A spiritual father's spirit is very important, the Lord told me. It is
with his spirit, sons and daughters learn to be disciplined in the things
of God. They learn how to carry the vision and mission that the Lord
has set before the men and women of God. It is in the spirit of a
spiritual father that sons and daughters develop a sense of confidence
in the Lord and are taught the value of the anointing of God on their
lives. It is with a spiritual father's spirit that the enemies of the sons'
and daughters' lives are dealt with, and sons and daughter are able to
walk in their destiny. A generation has come to a place where they
have given up the spiritual discipline they need in order to carry a
vision and accomplish the mission to have fame and popularity in
ministry. Leaders have given this generation the fame and the
"celebrity" of ministry and not the reality of it. The cross is something
that this generation must carry in order to fulfill the very mission of
God. Although we have been chosen to do great things in the earth for

the Lord, we have lost the discipline that is needed in order to be prepared to receive the mantle of the forefathers. This is a hard assignment for me because I am dealing with a generation who has become un-teachable and zealous without understanding. I have had to learn this coming up in ministry because I had to be mature to carry the vision and mission of God. I did not know what came along with the vision and mission, so a spiritual father had to teach me the way. This is what happened when it came to Elisha and Gehazi. Gehazi did not understand the season that he was in. His immaturity caused him to move before his time. Maturity is important to a spiritual father because it says that you have learned and have received understanding about a subject or a cause that has been taught or taken place. Learning how to follow in the Spirit and the sensitivity of the Spirit is important. Many leaders have lost this sensitivity and have passed this on to a generation that does what they want at any given time, not understanding that the Spirit of God leads us into that which is truth. Gehazi did not understand the sensitivity of the season that Prophet Elisha was in. He also had not gained understanding of Elisha's ministry. He had become full of what he could get in ministry and lost sight of Elisha's spirit. This means that Gehazi went in the power of his flesh, and he did not understand that that Elisha's spirit was with him. His ability not to understand that moved him to gain power by:

1. Questioning the motives of Elisha
2. Running after things
3. Lying on behalf of the Lord
4. Taking two young prophets with him
5. Going in his Father's spirit

These five things moved Gehazi to a place where he was willing to compromise his father's ministry in order to fit his needs. With all that had been given to Gehazi, he was positioned to carry on the legacy of Elisha's mantle, but because he despised the place of honor at which he had been placed, he lost the ministry he was destined to carry. Like so many young leaders in this generation, we have been destined to carry on the mantles of our forefathers, but because we have wanted the popularity of this life, we have chosen to give up those mantles to get things that would please us right now. This cannot be so. A generation of young people is depending on us to follow the proper protocol in order to receive the mantles that we will leave for them.

A Dead Man's Anointing

"Elisha died and was buried. Now Moabite raiders used to enter the country every spring. Once while some Israelites were burying a man, suddenly they saw a band of raiders; so they threw the man's body into Elisha's tomb. When the body touched Elisha's bones, the man came to life and stood up on his feet"
(2 Kings 13:20-21).

A generation that is now present must understand the importance of not thinking about self. As I sit here writing this book, I am more and more understanding of a people dying to themselves in order to fulfill the cause of the Kingdom. Therefore, the Lord allowed me to experience a trial that would break my heart. For years, I have been dealing with a daughter in my ministry about her character. I saw things in her that would make her a great leader, but I also saw the things inside her that would make her a bad leader. I was charged by the Lord to deal with her about these issues, but her pride was too much for God, me, and even herself. The Lord began to press me about her, and so I dealt with her about some character issues that I saw. Most people in our generation want the anointing without paying the price for it. Our generation wants everything quick and now. With this young lady, I saw the greed for power and popularity, but she did not have to character to handle such fame. She did not understand that with fame comes great character, and with great character comes great responsibility. The Lord was calling her to lead a generation of young people, but because she was not prepared, the Lord had placed her in my hands to deal with the pride that she blindly possessed. "A generation," the Lord said to me, "is blinded by themselves; they don't see that I have chosen them to be the ones to carry My Glory, to prepare the way for My Son." This generation does not see that it is too much of them. Like Gehazi, this generation sees only what they can get and not what they can give. Their passion for the world is heavy, and it has reached the depth of God's heart. This generation cannot cry out that they are outcasts to those that have said that they loved them, for the Lord has chosen the outcasts to do His will. I pushed this young lady to understand what the Lord had been calling her to do, but her heart harbored bitterness, and she wanted more than what she was getting. She felt lost and alone not knowing that God had positioned her there to birth her. Her frustration with her life only showed the Lord her immaturity to handle the weight of that which He wanted to give. But her complaints came before the Lord with disappointment. She never grasped the fact that she had to die to self in order to get the anointing, and the Lord refused to anoint a renegade with power. The renegade would only use that power to destroy others. The Lord had been dealing with me about our forefathers' mantles and the weight of the glory that was still in the grave. It was amazing to hear that the Glory of Lord still existed, but it is sad to hear that they are in the graves of holy men who never had a chance to pass them on. My heart has ached because my spiritual daughter did not understand the legacy that was left for us. She was so focused on the fame of life that she did not understand that the glory of the mantle came on a dead man. The scripture was clear that Elisha had died, and when he died, he died with the mantle of the prophetic on his life. Gehazi had lost it because he wanted something before his time. With Gehazi's disobedience came a curse from the prophet that left him unclean to carry the prophetic mantle, so the prophet died, and the mantle went with him. I know that our forefathers searched for young men and women of their time to carry their mantles, but they could not find any

123

who were willing to sacrifice self for that mantle. Generation, hear me well: you must give up everything to gain everything.

Elisha had been in his grave, and scripture tells us about a man who had died. This man was getting ready to be buried in a tomb that had nothing in it. For him and his family, his death may have been meaningless and his life a vain one, but that day, his death caused him to get a mantle. The Bible says that they threw the man into the tomb of Elisha, and his body touched the bones of Elisha, and he became a living soul. From that day, that man had purpose; from that day, that man possessed something greater than himself. He possessed the anointing of a prophet that he probably had not met nor had seen, but he surely had heard of. That day, his death had birthed a cause; for that day, a dead man received the mantle of the prophet.

CHAPTER 11
REVIVAL FIRE

"And afterward, I will pour out my Spirit on all people. Your sons and daughters will prophesy, your old men will dream dreams, your young men will see visions. Even on my servants, both men and women, I will pour out my Spirit in those days. I will show wonders in the heavens and on the earth, blood and fire and billows of smoke. The sun will be turned to darkness and the moon to blood before the coming of the great and dreadful day of the Lord. And everyone who calls on the name of the LORD will be saved; for on Mount Zion and in Jerusalem there will be deliverance, as the LORD has said, among the survivors whom the LORD calls" Joel 2:28-32

It was July 2, 2008, and the Lord had sent us to San Juan, Puerto Rico. The young people whom we had trained for over two years had been prepared to take on the world. The Lord had told me before we got to San Juan that He was going to allow the young people to experience His presence there. "It is here," the Lord said, "that I am going to confirm My choice of those who were called to be a part of Joel's Army." I was excited, but I did not know what the Lord had in store and how much that night would change me. We had landed in San Juan on July 1, 2008. A few of my leaders and I went to pick up the rental van. When we got there, the Holy Spirit spoke to me to check our accounts. I told my Chief Financial Officer to do so. As he was calling, I was at the rental car check-out counter preparing the paper work. My Chief Financial Officer came back over to me and said, "Prophet, the money in the bank is gone." We immediately called the bank and found out what had happened. We called the place where the error had occurred, but the money was not returned. At that moment, I became puzzled, and we began to search for money. I prayed to the Lord right there and went to the check -out counter to finish the paper work. The Customer Service Representative said that our van was ready, and all we had to do was go and pick it out. He told me right there not to worry about anything; my card would not be charged until I returned the vehicles. We were relieved at what had happened and began to pick up the young leaders from the airport. As we got to the place where we were staying, we looked and saw how beautiful the house we were staying in was. But there was a major problem: the water did not work, and the house had no furniture, not even any beds. We had been truly sent on a mission trip. We looked over in the corner, and to our amazement, there were some Army cots that we had to put together; this was a sign from the Lord that he was raising up His Army. Now in order for the young people to understand their new-found journey, they had to live like the Army in the natural. The Lord had been speaking, and we had to set up camp in the middle of a country that we would do battle with. The Lord had sent us to San Juan to deal with seven spirits that held that country captive. Those spirits were:

1. Homosexuality

2. Poverty

3. Religion

4. Suicide

5. Witchcraft

6. Sickness

7. Sexual immorality

These spirits were a nuisance to the island of San Juan, and the Lord had sent an Army there to deal with them. We finally settled in the camp, and the morning had come; we all got up with great anticipation because we did not know what would come before us. We arrived at the church to do a teaching with the people and to prepare for their Wednesday Night Service. We began to meet the people of the church and fell in love with the hospitality of the people there. The time had come for the night service to begin, and I was nervous. I don't speak Spanish and was not used to having an interpreter; however, the people there could understand a little English, so it made it a lot easier for me. As I began to lead praise and worship, I started to smell smoke in the building, but there was no fire. The smoke began to get thicker, and my eyes began to burn like I was in a burning building. Before I knew it, I was blind. My eyes became a torch of fire, and I could see in the Spirit Realm what the Lord wanted for His people. I yelled out to my staff, "I am blind! I cannot see!" No one believed me, so I yelled again, and one of the young men who was with me came to see about me. As he began to guide me under the power of the Holy Ghost, the Lord possessed me, and I began to see the issues of the people that were at hand. The issues that were in the spirit were so detailed. I had not experienced this anointing before. What is more amazing about this is that I never spoke the people's language, yet when the Holy Spirit began to talk, the language barrier didn't matter. The people had a need that day, and the Lord had met us there. The people began to fall under the power of the Holy Ghost, and the presence of God was like a fiery furnace. The Lord spoke to me and said, "Take the towel in your hand and throw it on Joel's Army." I looked at the Army and said, "Today, the Lord will use you all mightily. The minute this towel hits you all the anointing of God will fall on you." As the towel was released, I saw the Power of God fall on the young people and as they walked past the people, the people began to fall under the power without even being touched. It was so amazing that the young people were in awe, with a confused look on their faces. They began to minister to the people, and I began to walk outside to get some air; the mantle had fallen, and the young people had now received the Fire for Revival. That day, the Lord had taken a bunch of young people who had been rejected, tossed to the side and called "Outcasts" and poured out His Spirit on them. That day, the young people became a sign and the first fruit of their generation to receive the mantle of their fathers and an anointing to change the world. That day, the Outcasts became God's prophets and a Holy Army for their generation!

Reference Page

1. All scripture have been taken from the NIV and New King James Bible.

2. Some definitions have been taken from Webster Dictionary

3. Some definitions have been taken from: http://www.thefreedictionary.com

4. Some definitions have been taken from http://dictionary.reference.com

5. Some definitions have been taken from http://mw1.meriam-webster.com

6. Tyndale Bible Dictionary, Walter A. Elwell, Ph.D and Philip W. Comfort, Ph.D, Tyndale House Publishers Wheaton Illinois.

7. Holman Illustrated Bible Dictionary, Trent C. Butler, Nashville Tennessee.

8. Nelson's New Illustrated Bible Dictionary, Ronald F.Youngblood, Thomas Nelson Publishers, 1995, 1986.

9. The Prophet's Dictionary, Paula A. Price, PH.D, Whitaker House.

ABOUT PROPHET KEEAN SUTTON

Prophet Keean Sutton is the Founder, CEO, and Senior Pastor of Vigor Youth Ministries International. Born in the inner city of Chicago, Illinois, Keean Sutton faced humble beginnings and a poverty-stricken atmosphere that beckoned for his very soul. Still, this man of God escaped his hellish beginnings to go about the will of the Lord, which included gathering a group of chosen teenagers to stand in the midst of a conflagration that would heat up the world in anticipation of the Kingdom of God. With this in mind, VIGOR, (meaning Victory In God Our Redeemer) was birthed and the fire God would be nothing but extraordinary on lives of young people that would encounter this man of God.

He has been called to develop leaders, shape youth ministries, and bring revelation to young people across the world. The mantle that Pastor Keean carries is one of great purpose and zeal, as he has been called to be a prophet to his generation. With the mantle of the prophetic, he has been called to shape the lives of young people and prepare a generation to be ready to carry the mantle of their forefathers.

He is a graduate of Beulah Heights University and is carrying a Bachelor degree in Biblical Education and a Masters Degree in Administration and Leadership He is also pursing a Master Degree in Youth Ministry Leadership at Huntington University.

He is the founder of Joel's Army, a group of young leaders from different churches around the world, The Nehemiah Connection, a ministry which caters to the needs of Youth Pastors and Youth Leaders, and is the Co-Founder of Prophecy Productions and the Author of the New Books Outcast and 20 Laws of Youth Ministry.

He is married to Wynkia Sutton has two children, Miracle and Josiah, and a host of spiritual sons and daughters. Pastor Keean's passion and sincerity for young people speaks volume through his life and ministry. His is missions is clear, to train, build, and develop young leaders to affect their generation.

For booking information or to contact Pastor Keean Sutton or Vigor Youth Ministries please visit www.vigoryouthministries.org or www.kindlethefireministries.com.

Made in the USA
Charleston, SC
22 March 2014